T0057096

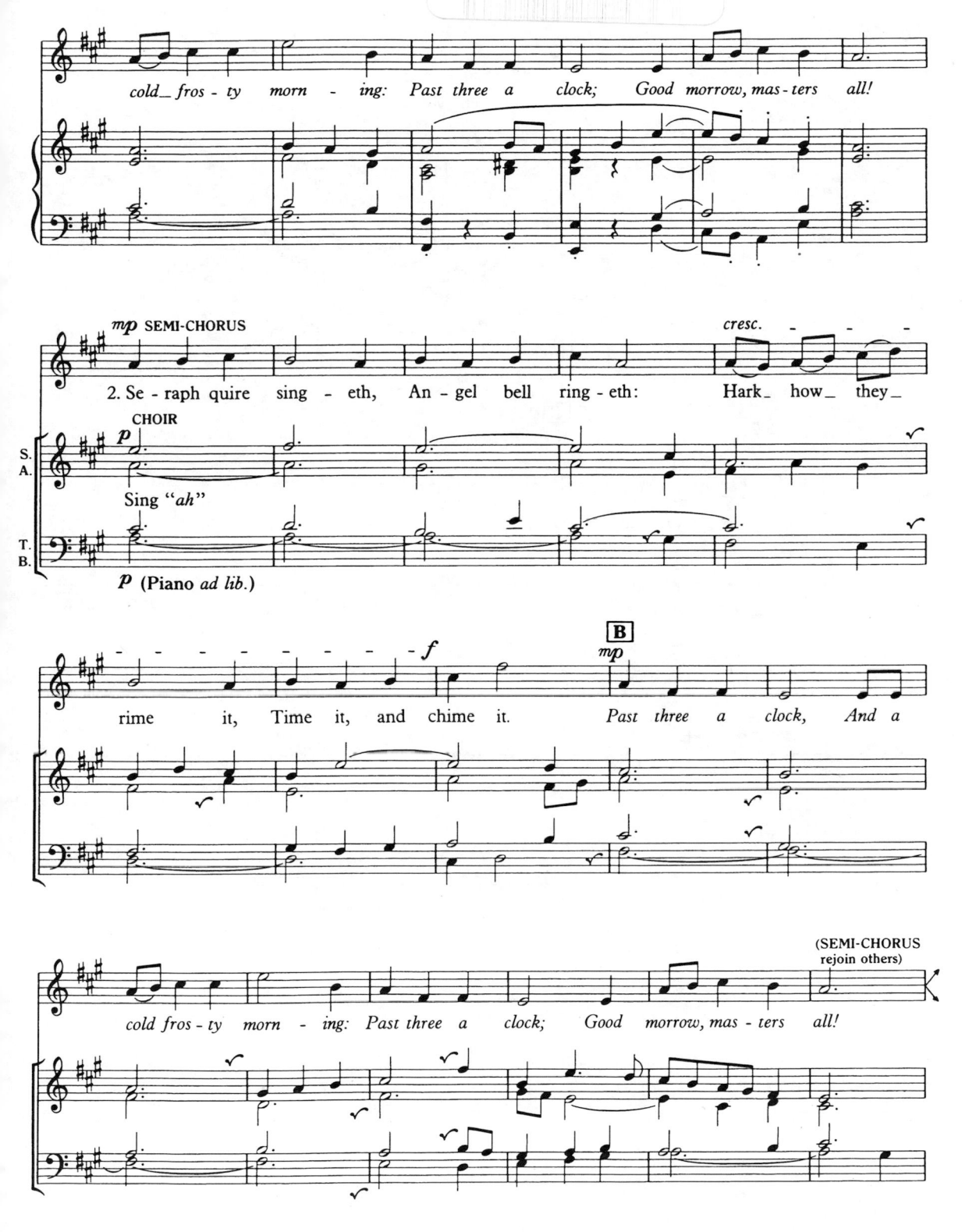
cold_ fros - ty morn - ing: Past three a clock; Good morrow, mas - ters all!
mp SEMI-CHORUS
cresc.
2. Se - raph quire sing - eth, An - gel bell ring - eth: Hark_ how_ they_
CHOIR
p
S.
A.
Sing "ah"
T.
B.
p (Piano ad lib.)
f
B
mp
rime it, Time it, and chime it. Past three a clock, And a
(SEMI-CHORUS rejoin others)
cold fros - ty morn - ing: Past three a clock; Good morrow, mas - ters all!

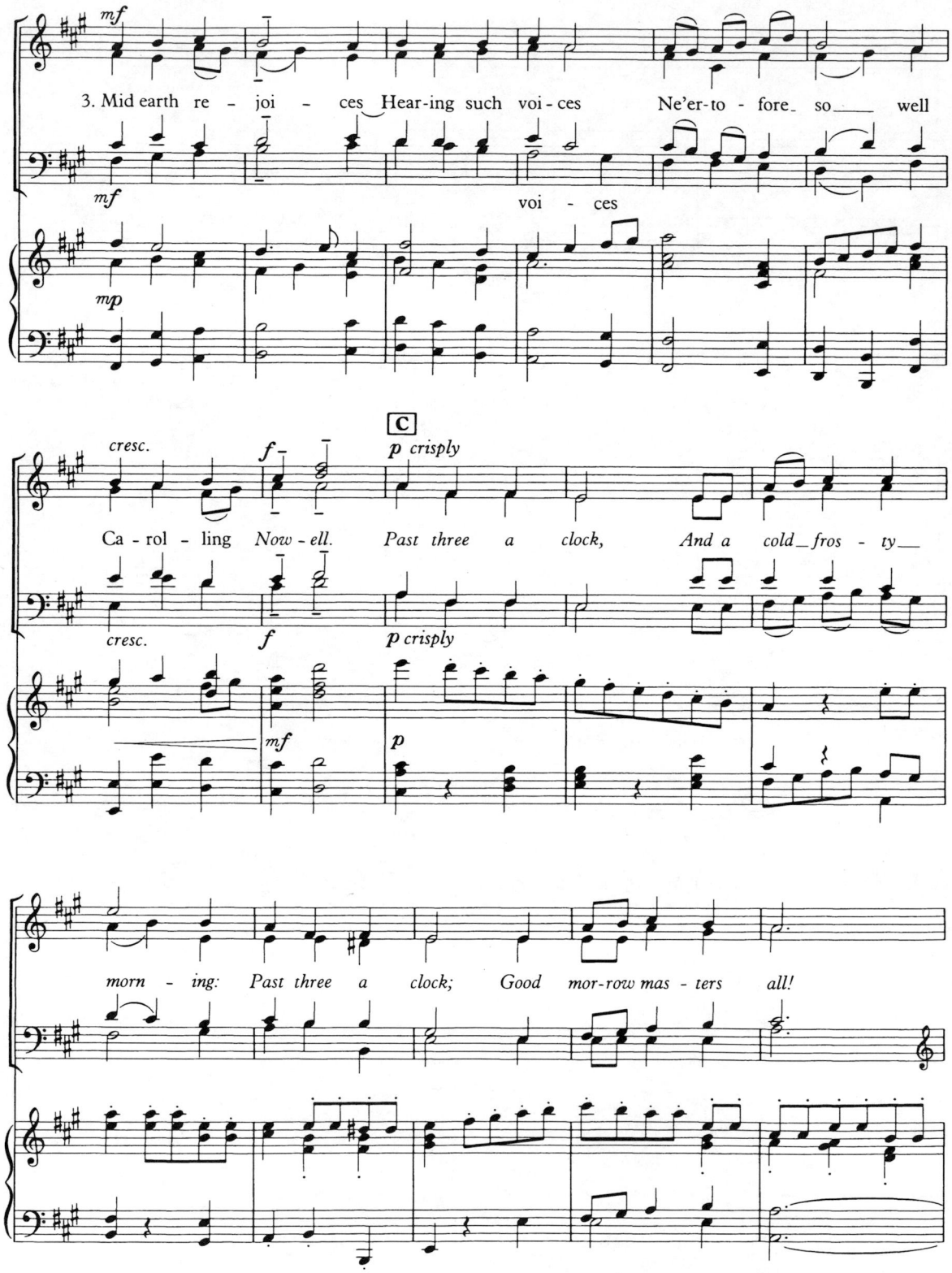
mf
3. Mid earth re - joi - ces Hear-ing such voi-ces Ne'er-to - fore so well
mf
voi - ces
mp
C
cresc.
f
p crisply
Ca - rol - ling Now - ell. Past three a clock, And a cold fros - ty
cresc.
f
p crisply
mf
p
morn - ing: Past three a clock; Good mor-row mas - ters all!

OXFORD

Twelve Christmas Carols

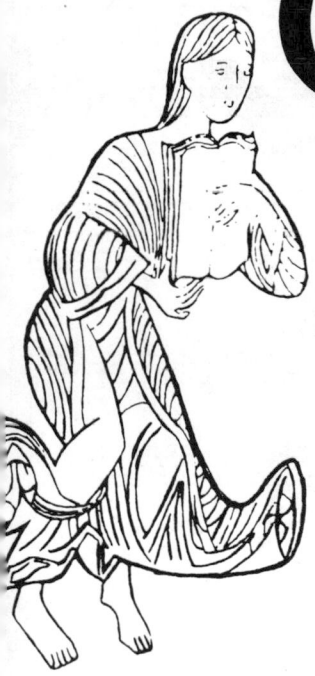

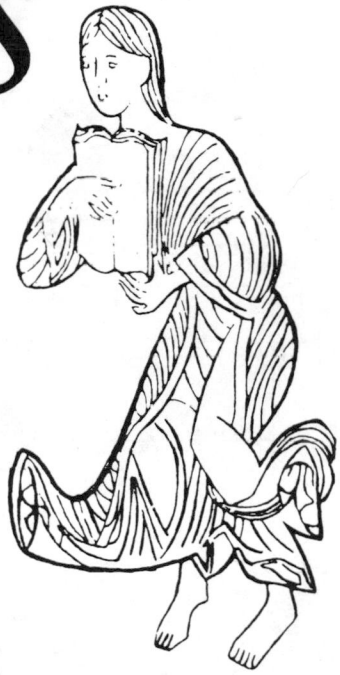

in two sets

SET 2

Past three a clock
Away in a manger
Gabriel's Message
Noel nouvelet
Sans Day Carol
The coming of our King

arranged for mixed voices and orchestra
or piano by

John Rutter

TWELVE CHRISTMAS CAROLS

arranged by JOHN RUTTER

SET 2

1. PAST THREE A CLOCK

G. R. Woodward
(refrain traditional)

English traditional carol

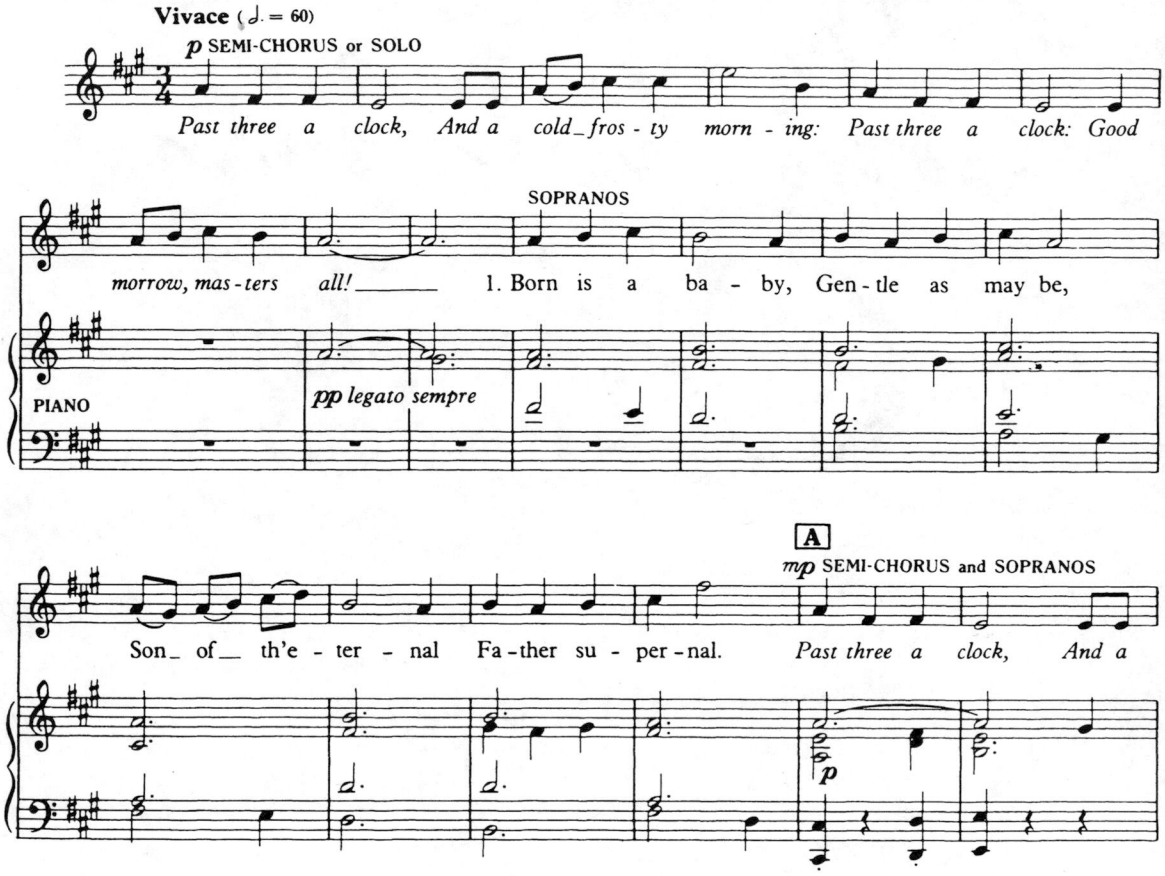

Set 1: *Here we come a-wassailing; The Infant King; Shepherds' Noel; Quittez, pasteurs; Stille Nacht; O come, O come Immanuel*

The twelve carols have been recorded by the Clare College Singers and Orchestra on HMV CLP/CSD 3670 (for release in 1970).

Orchestral scores and parts are on hire.

Note: Piano accompaniments are not always identical with their orchestral counterparts.

Instrumentation for *Past three a clock*: 2 flutes, 2 oboes, bassoon, 2 horns, percussion (1 player), harp (opt.), and strings

Also on sale: *Eight Christmas Carols* arranged by John Rutter, in 2 sets, recorded by the Clare College Singers and Orchestra on HMV CLP/CSD 3634

The words of *Past three a clock* are from *The Cambridge Carol Book* and are reprinted by kind permission of the S.P.C.K.

© Oxford University Press 1969

Printed in U.S.
OXFORD UNIVERSITY PRESS, MUSIC DEPARTMENT, GREAT CLARENDON STREET, OXFORD OX2 6DP

Photocopying this copyright material is ILLEGAL.

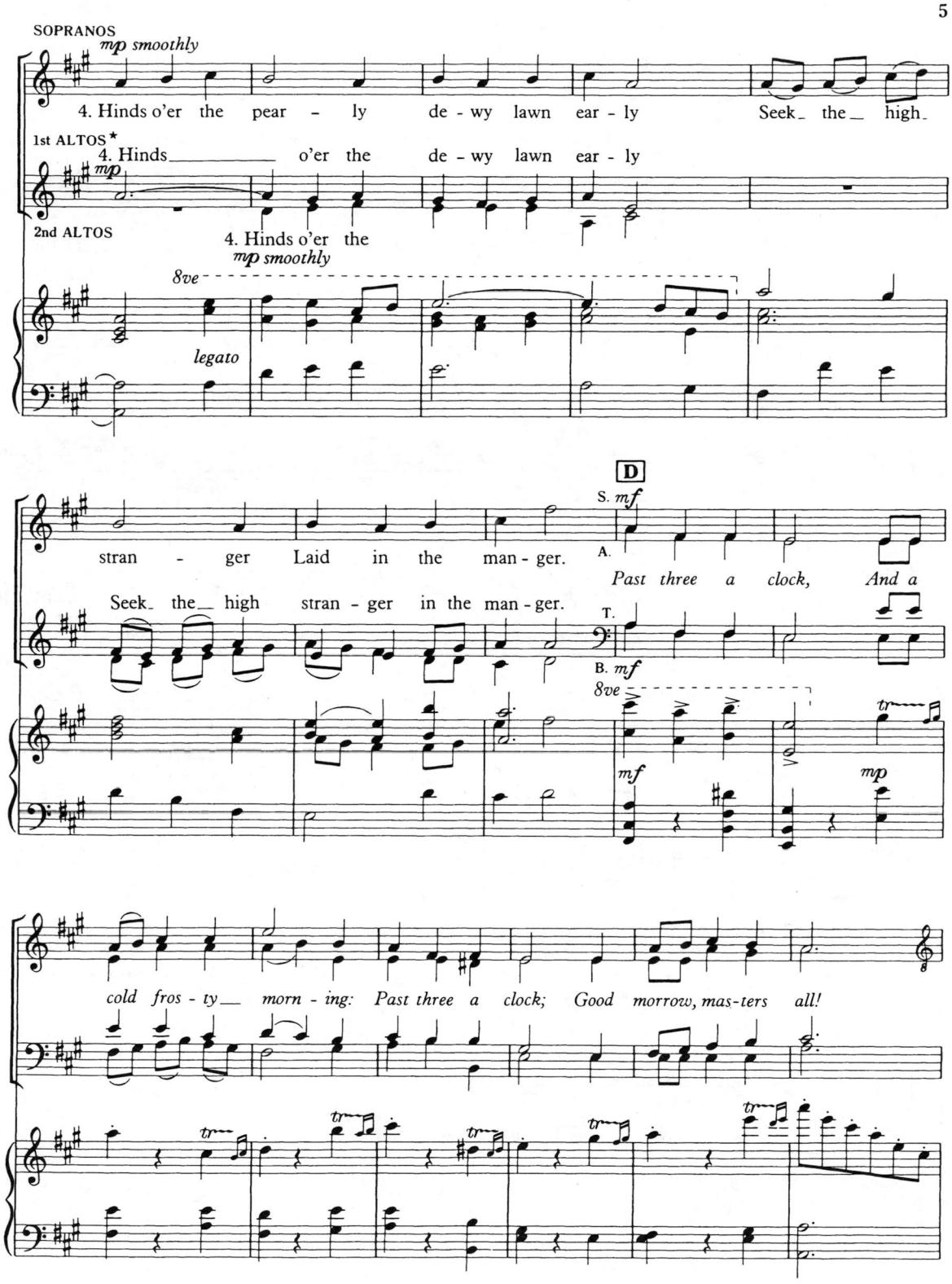

*or 2nd sopranos

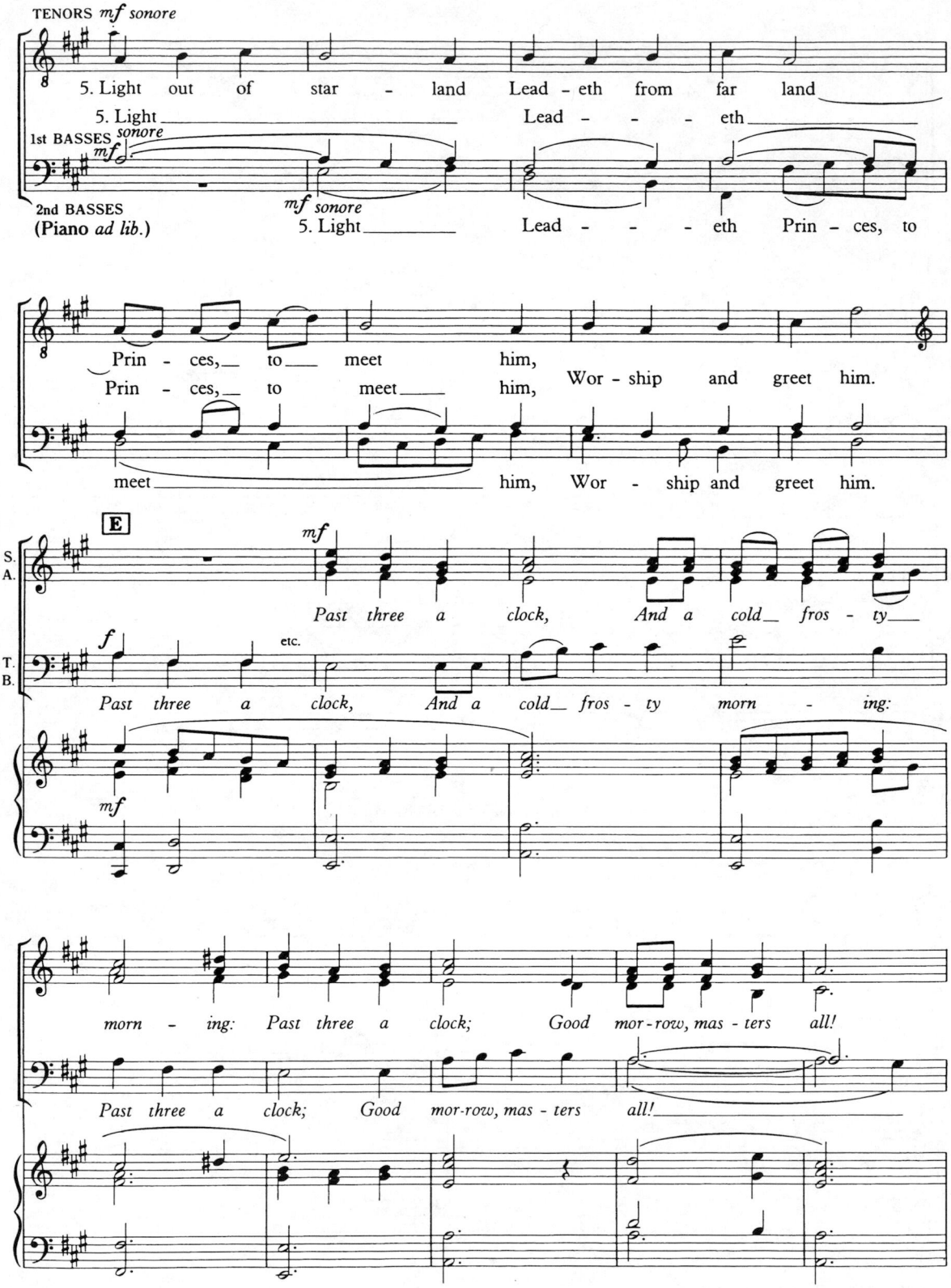
TENORS mf sonore
5. Light out of star - land Lead - eth from far land
5. Light Lead - - - eth
1st BASSES mf sonore
2nd BASSES
(Piano ad lib.)
mf sonore
5. Light Lead - - - eth Prin - ces, to
Prin - ces, to meet him,
Prin - ces, to meet him, Wor - ship and greet him.
meet him, Wor - ship and greet him.
E
S.
A.
mf
Past three a clock, And a cold fros - ty
T.
B.
f
etc.
Past three a clock, And a cold fros - ty morn - ing:
mf
morn - ing: Past three a clock; Good mor-row, mas - ters all!
Past three a clock; Good mor-row, mas - ters all!

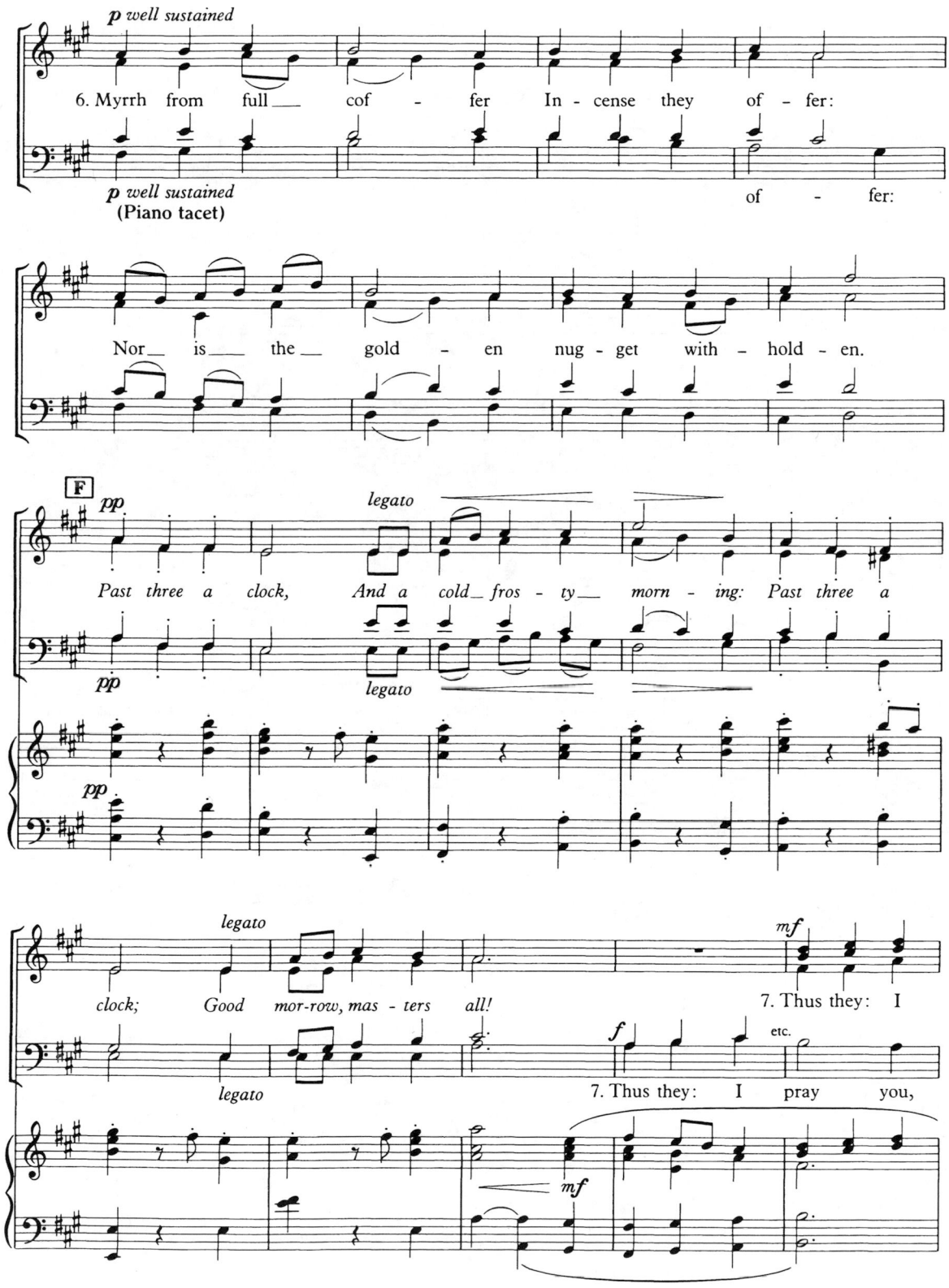
p well sustained
6. Myrrh from full cof - fer In - cense they of - fer:
p well sustained
(Piano tacet)
of - fer:
Nor is the gold - en nug - get with - hold - en.
F
pp
legato
Past three a clock, And a cold fros - ty morn - ing: Past three a
pp
legato
pp
legato
clock; Good mor-row, mas - ters all!
mf
7. Thus they: I
f
etc.
legato
7. Thus they: I pray you,
mf

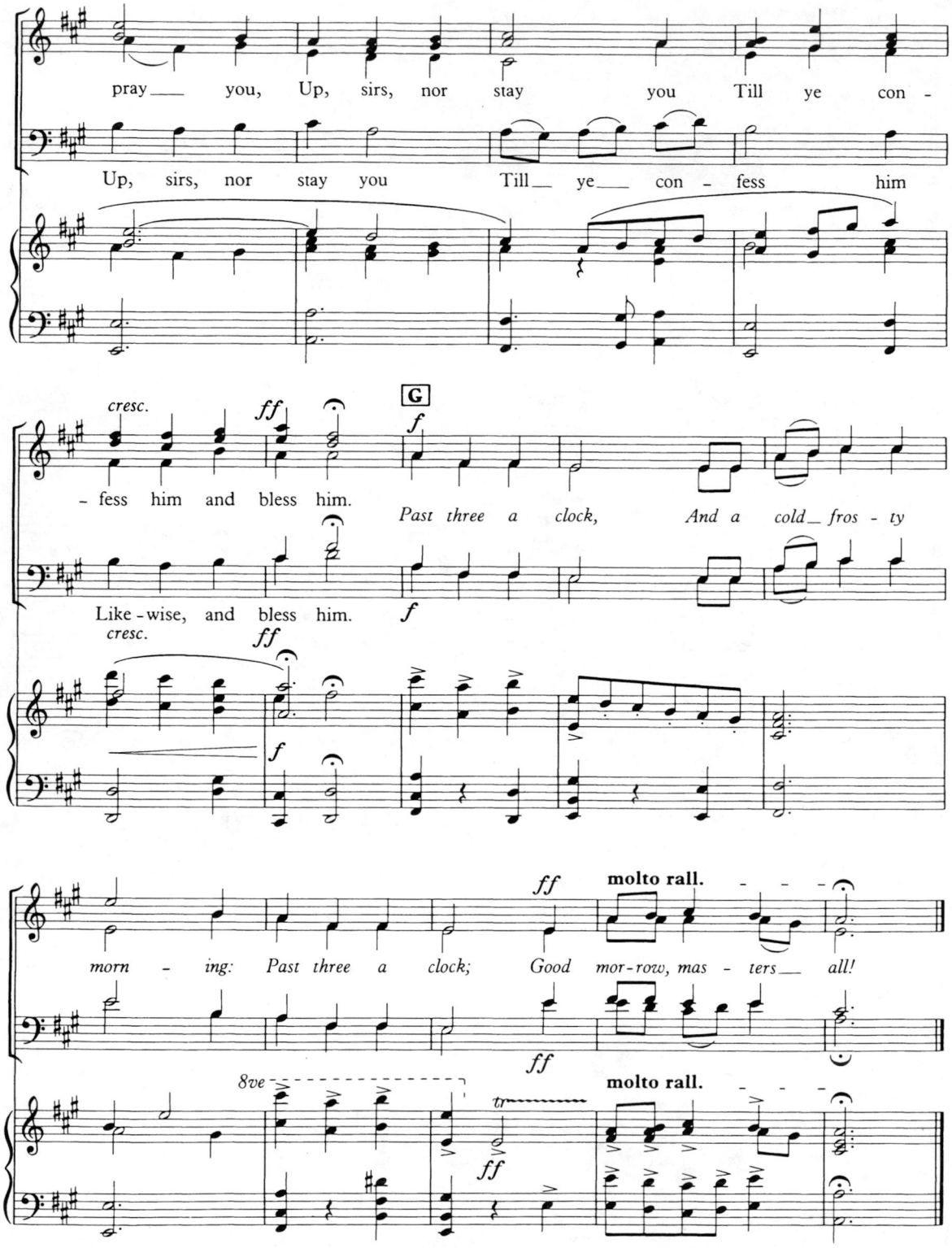
pray you, Up, sirs, nor stay you Till ye con -
Up, sirs, nor stay you Till ye con - fess him
cresc.
ff
G
f
- fess him and bless him.
Past three a clock, And a cold fros - ty
Like - wise, and bless him.
f
cresc.
ff
f
ff
molto rall.
morn - ing: Past three a clock; Good mor - row, mas - ters all!
ff
8ve
tr
ff
molto rall.

2. AWAY IN A MANGER

Words anon. W. J. Kirkpatrick

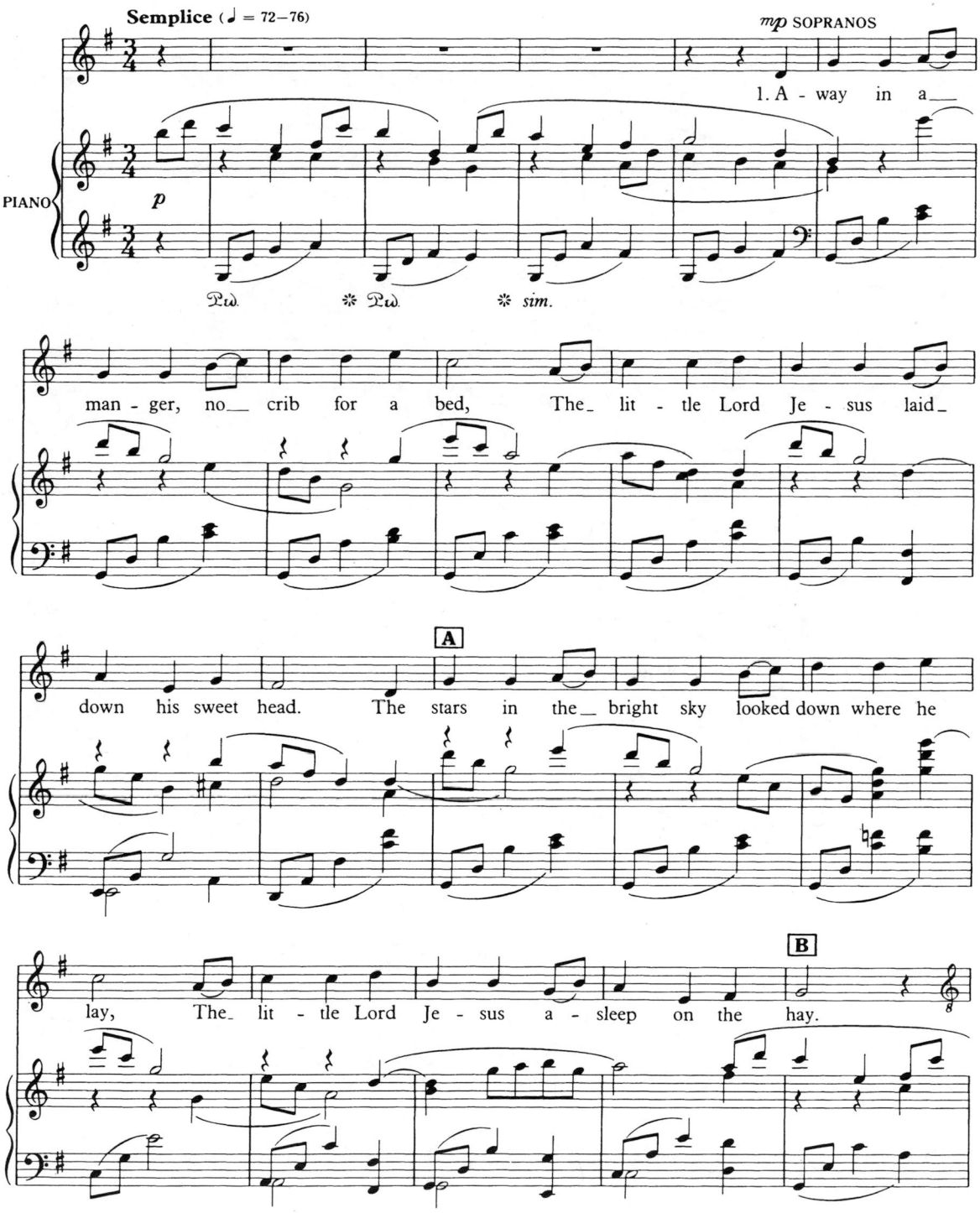

Instrumentation: Flute, oboe, bassoon, 2 horns, harp, and strings

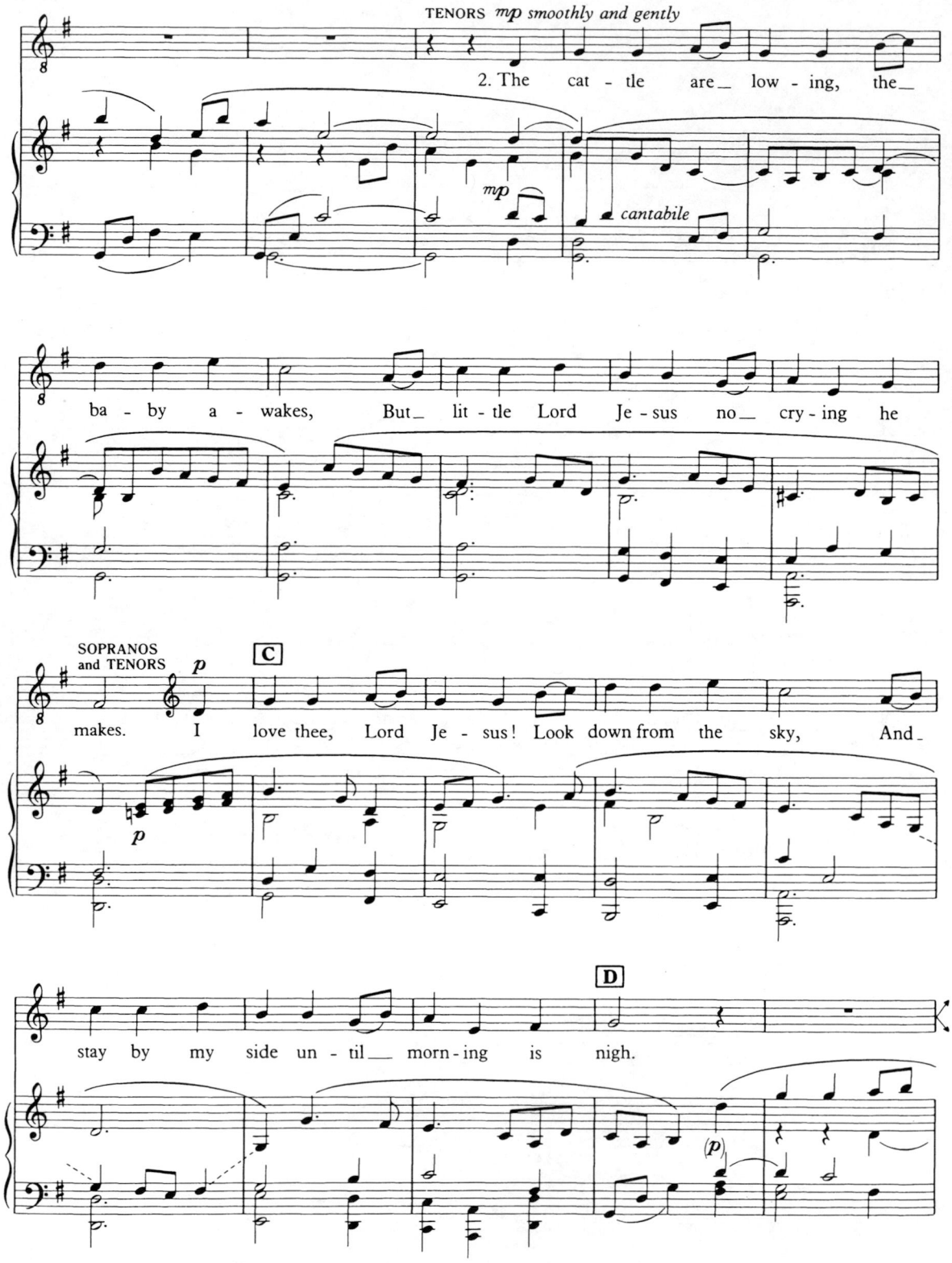
TENORS mp smoothly and gently
2. The cat - tle are low - ing, the
mp
cantabile
ba - by a - wakes, But lit - tle Lord Je - sus no cry - ing he
SOPRANOS and TENORS
p
C
makes. I love thee, Lord Je - sus! Look down from the sky, And
p
D
stay by my side un - til morn - ing is nigh.
(p)

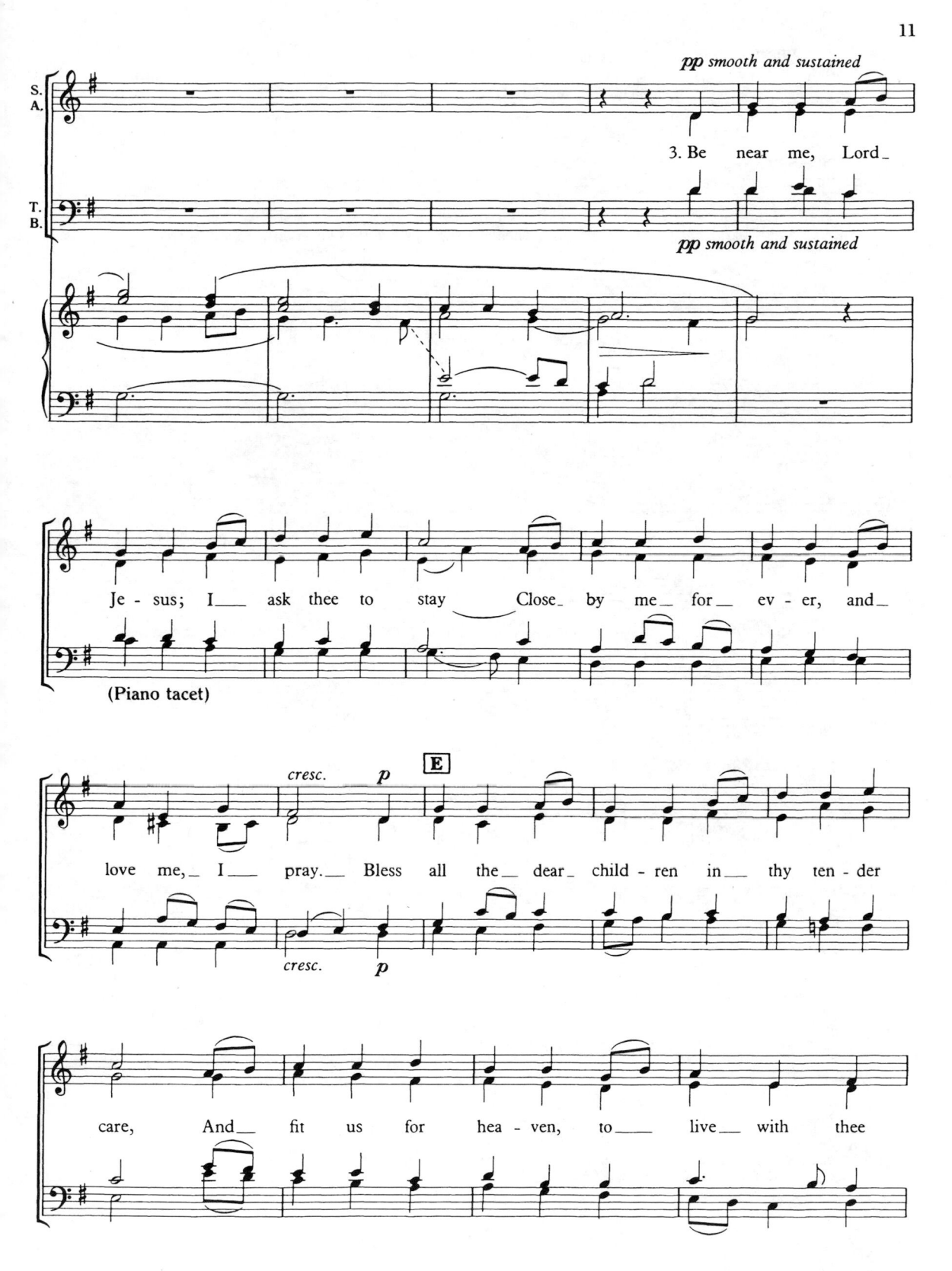
pp smooth and sustained
S.
A.
3. Be near me, Lord
T.
B.
pp smooth and sustained
Je - sus; I ask thee to stay Close by me for ev - er, and
(Piano tacet)
cresc.
p
E
love me, I pray. Bless all the dear child - ren in thy ten - der
cresc.
p
care, And fit us for hea - ven, to live with thee

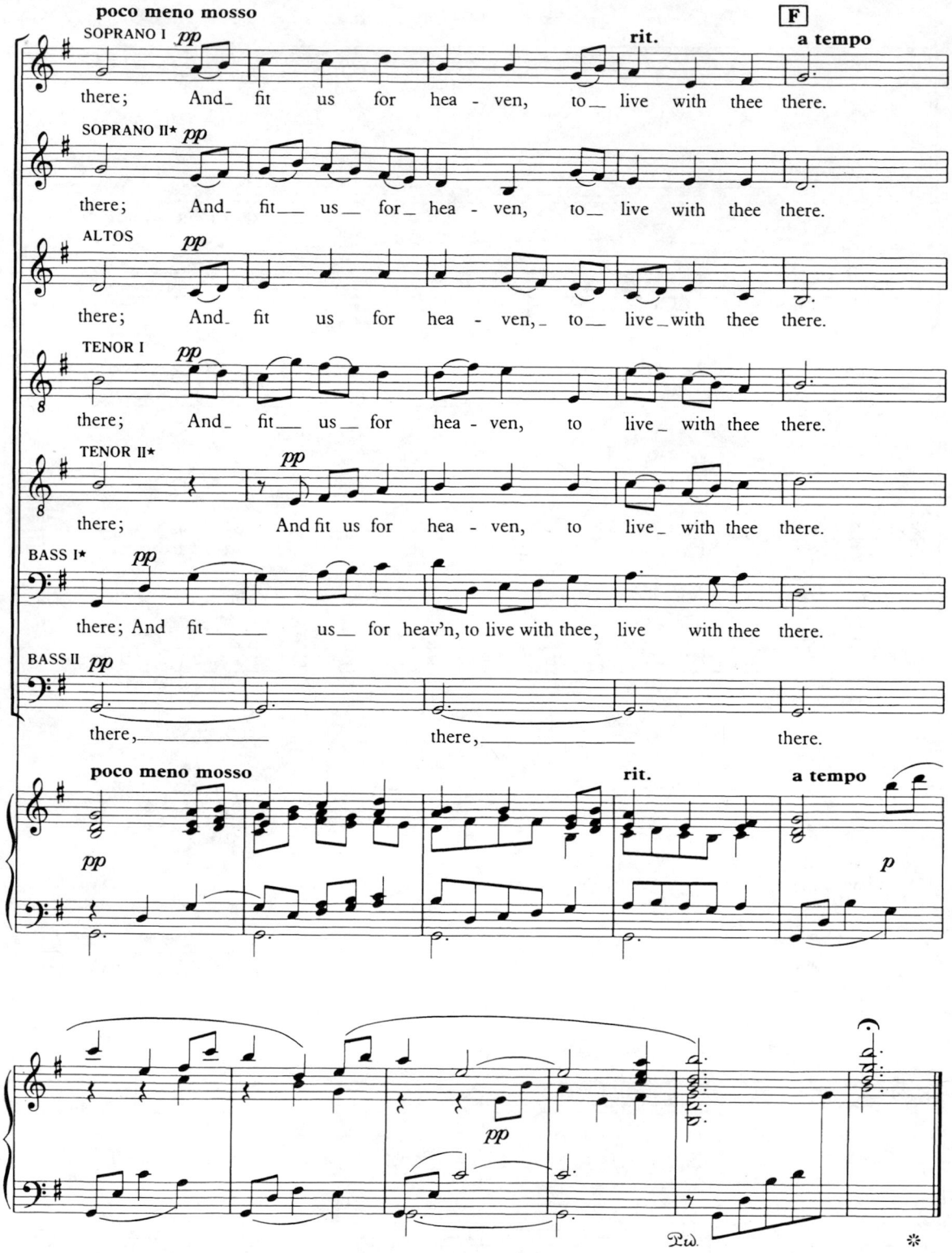

* If absolutely necessary, these parts may be omitted

3. GABRIEL'S MESSAGE

S. Baring-Gould

Basque carol

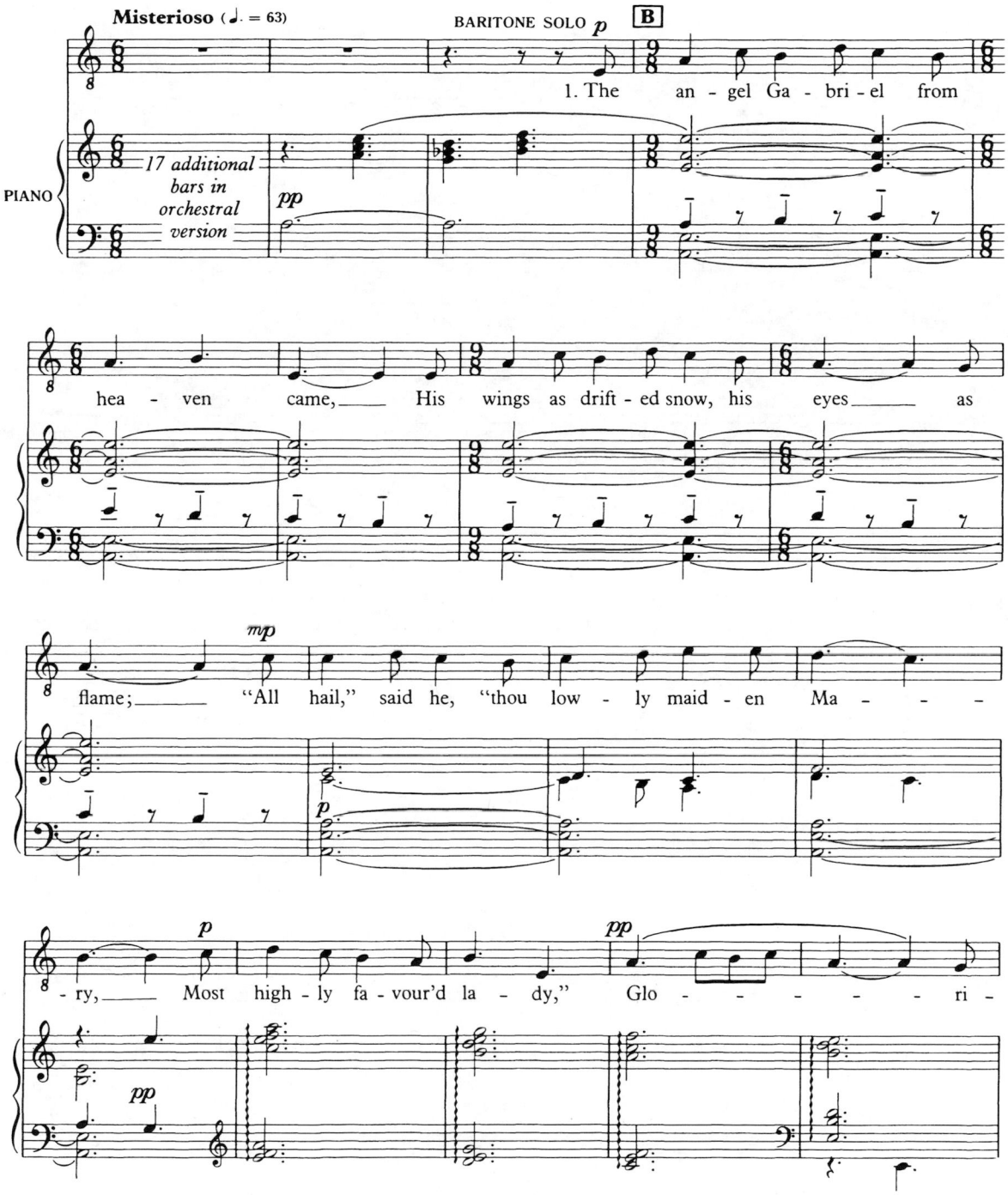

Melody and words reprinted by permission of H. Freeman & Co.
Instrumentation: Flute (doubling piccolo), 2 oboes, bassoon, 2 horns, harp, and strings

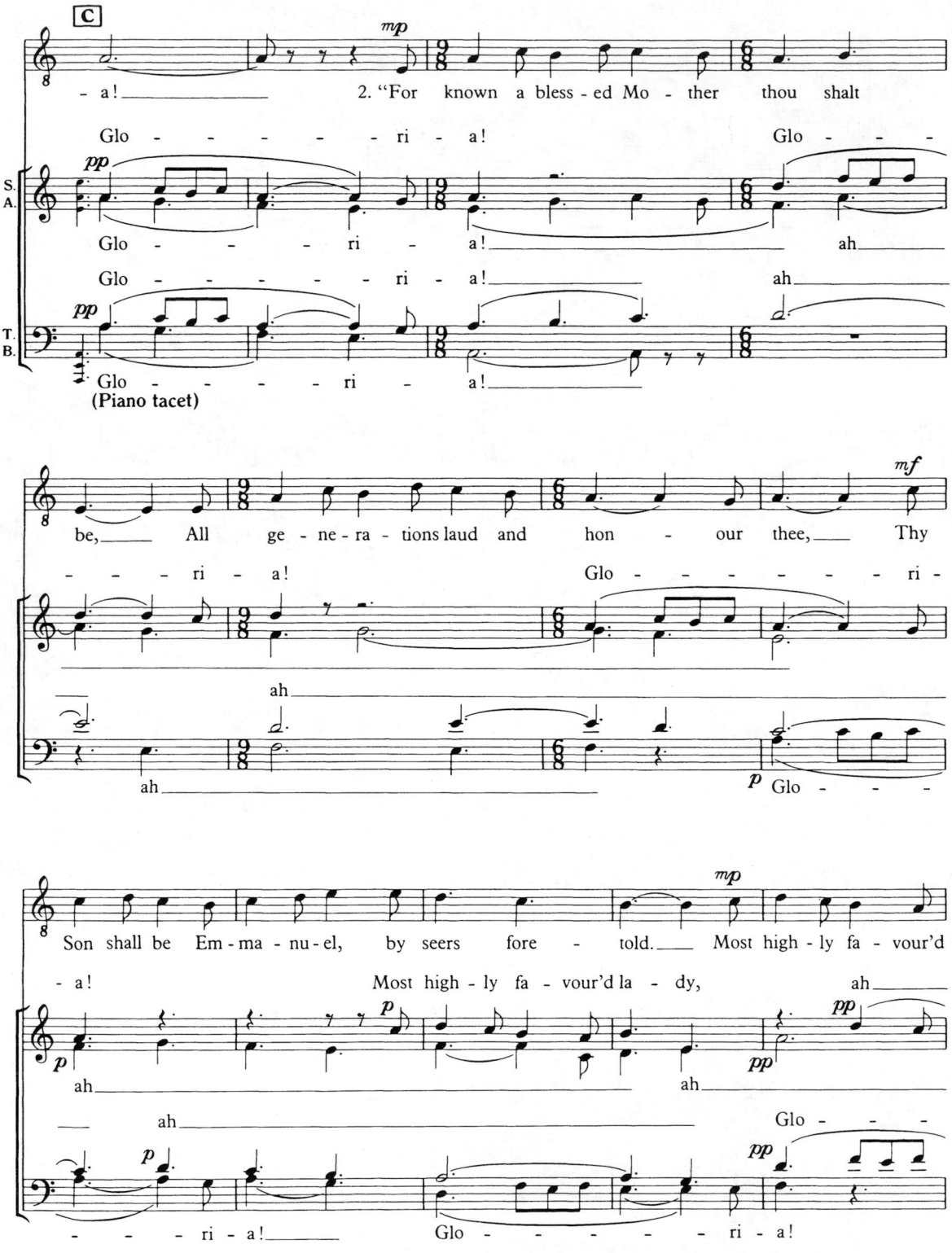
C
mp
- a! 2. "For known a bless - ed Mo - ther thou shalt
Glo - - - - - - ri - a! Glo - - -
S.
A.
pp
Glo - - - ri - a! ah
Glo - - - - - - ri - a! ah
T.
B.
pp
Glo - - - - - ri - a!
(Piano tacet)
be, All ge - ne - ra - tions laud and hon - our thee, Thy
mf
- - - ri - a! Glo - - - - - - - ri -
ah
ah
p
Glo - - -
Son shall be Em - ma - nu - el, by seers fore - told. Most high - ly fa - vour'd
mp
- a! Most high - ly fa - vour'd la - dy, ah
p
pp
ah ah
ah Glo - - -
p
pp
- - - ri - a! Glo - - - - - - ri - a!

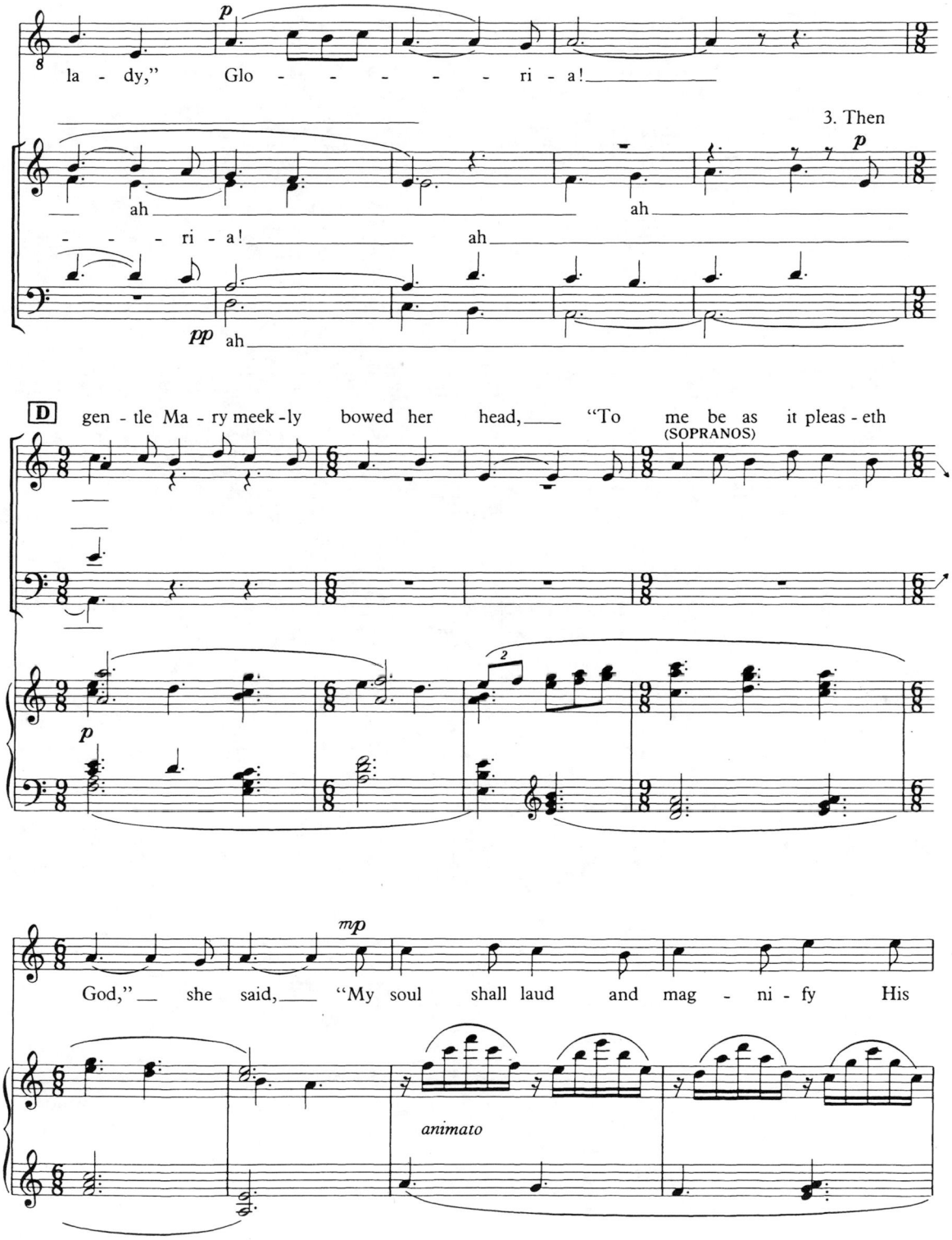
p
la - dy," Glo - - - - - - ri - a!
3. Then
p
ah ah
- - - ri - a! ah
pp ah
D
gen - tle Ma - ry meek - ly bowed her head, "To me be as it pleas - eth
(SOPRANOS)
p
mp
God," she said, "My soul shall laud and mag - ni - fy His
animato

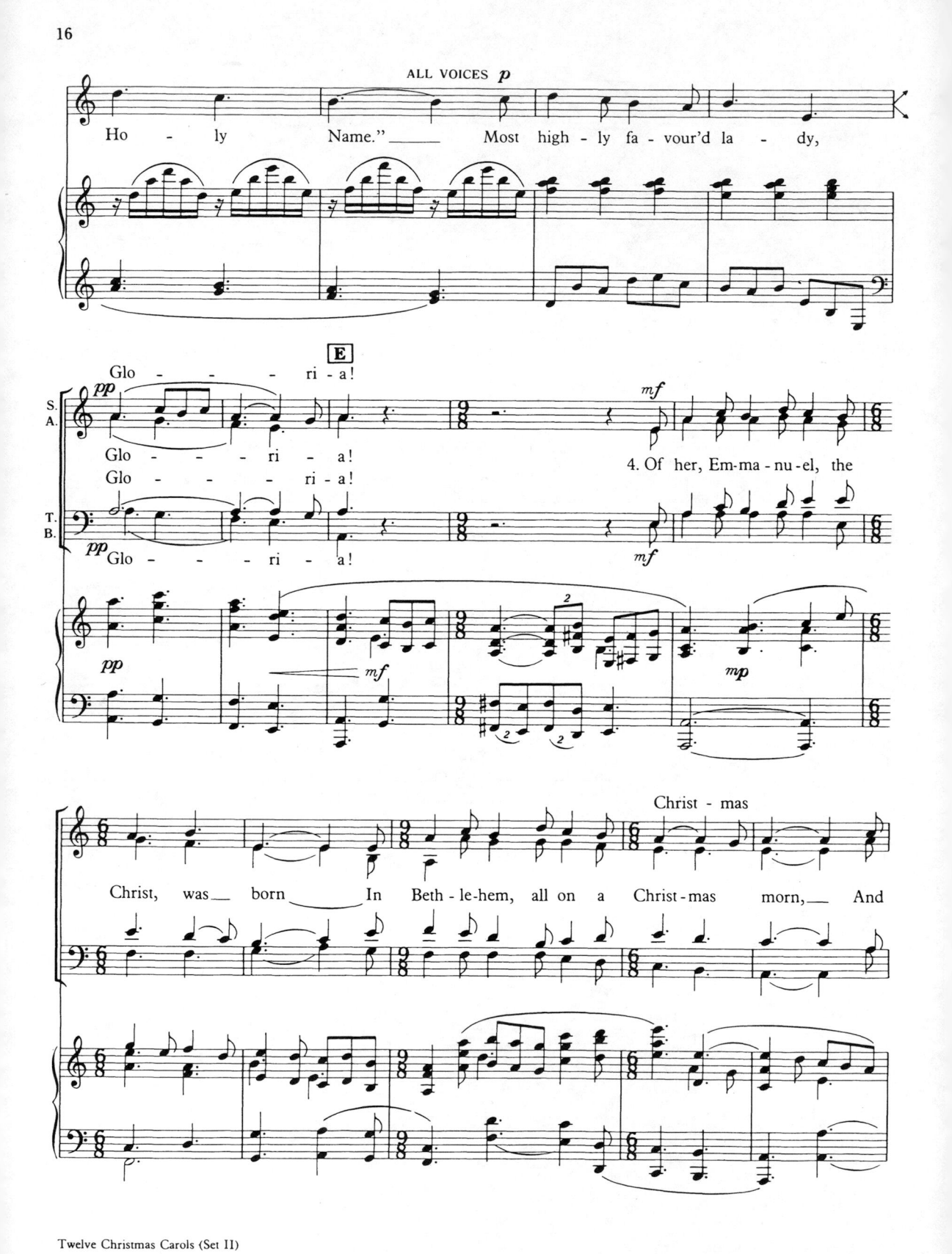
ALL VOICES p
Ho - ly Name." Most high - ly fa - vour'd la - dy,
E
Glo - - - ri - a!
pp
S.
A.
Glo - - - ri - a!
Glo - - - ri - a!
mf
4. Of her, Em-ma - nu - el, the
T.
B.
pp Glo - - - ri - a!
mf
pp
mf
mp
Christ - mas
Christ, was born In Beth - le-hem, all on a Christ - mas morn, And

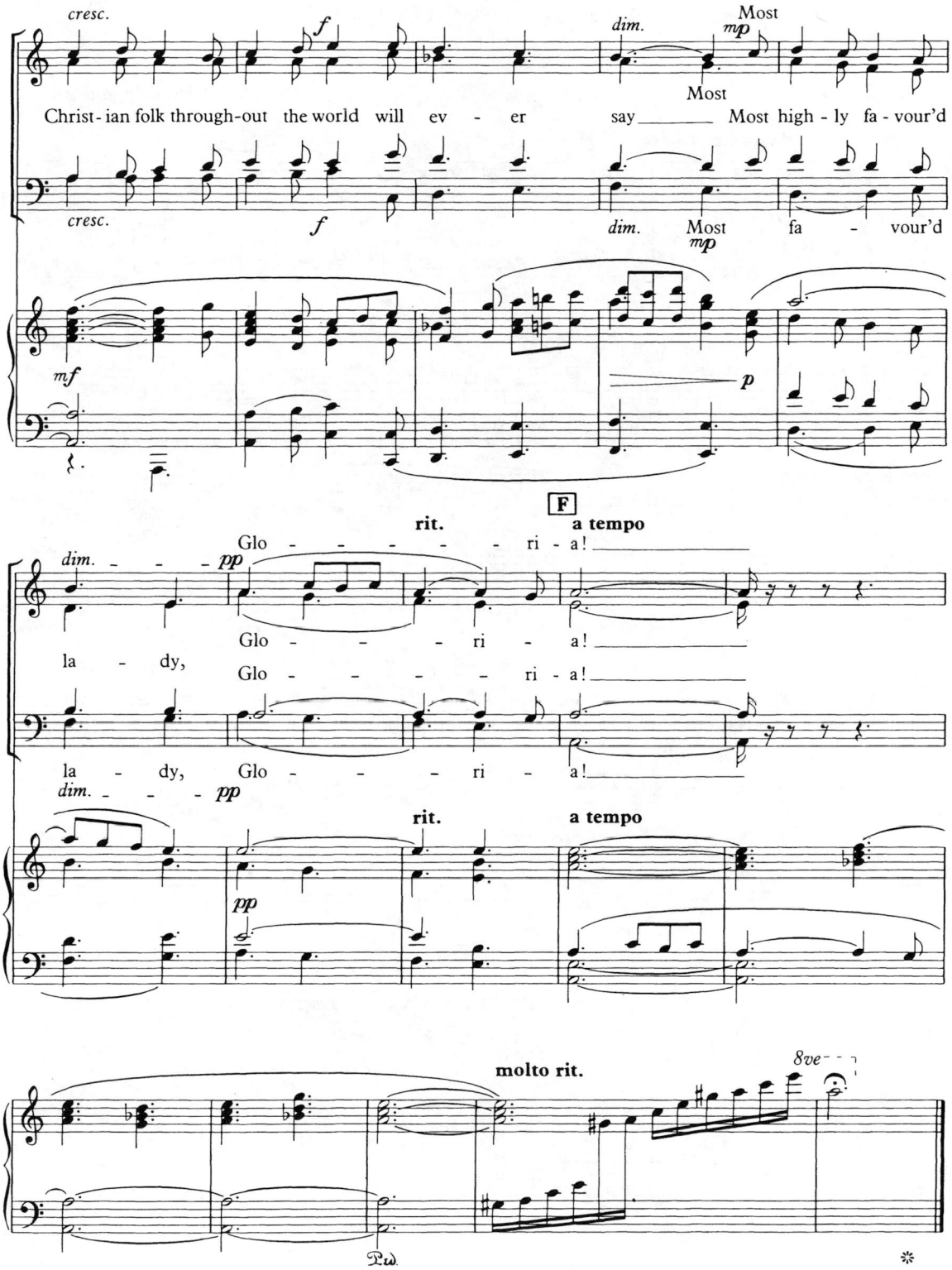
cresc.
f
dim.
mp
Most
Christ-ian folk through-out the world will ev - er say Most high - ly fa - vour'd
cresc.
f
dim.
Most fa - vour'd
mp
mf
p
F
rit.
a tempo
Glo - - - - - ri - a!
dim.
pp
Glo - - - ri - a!
la - dy,
Glo - - - - ri - a!
la - dy, Glo - - - ri - a!
dim.
pp
rit.
a tempo
pp
molto rit.
8ve

4. NOËL NOUVELET

(Nowell, sing nowell)

English words J. R.

French traditional carol

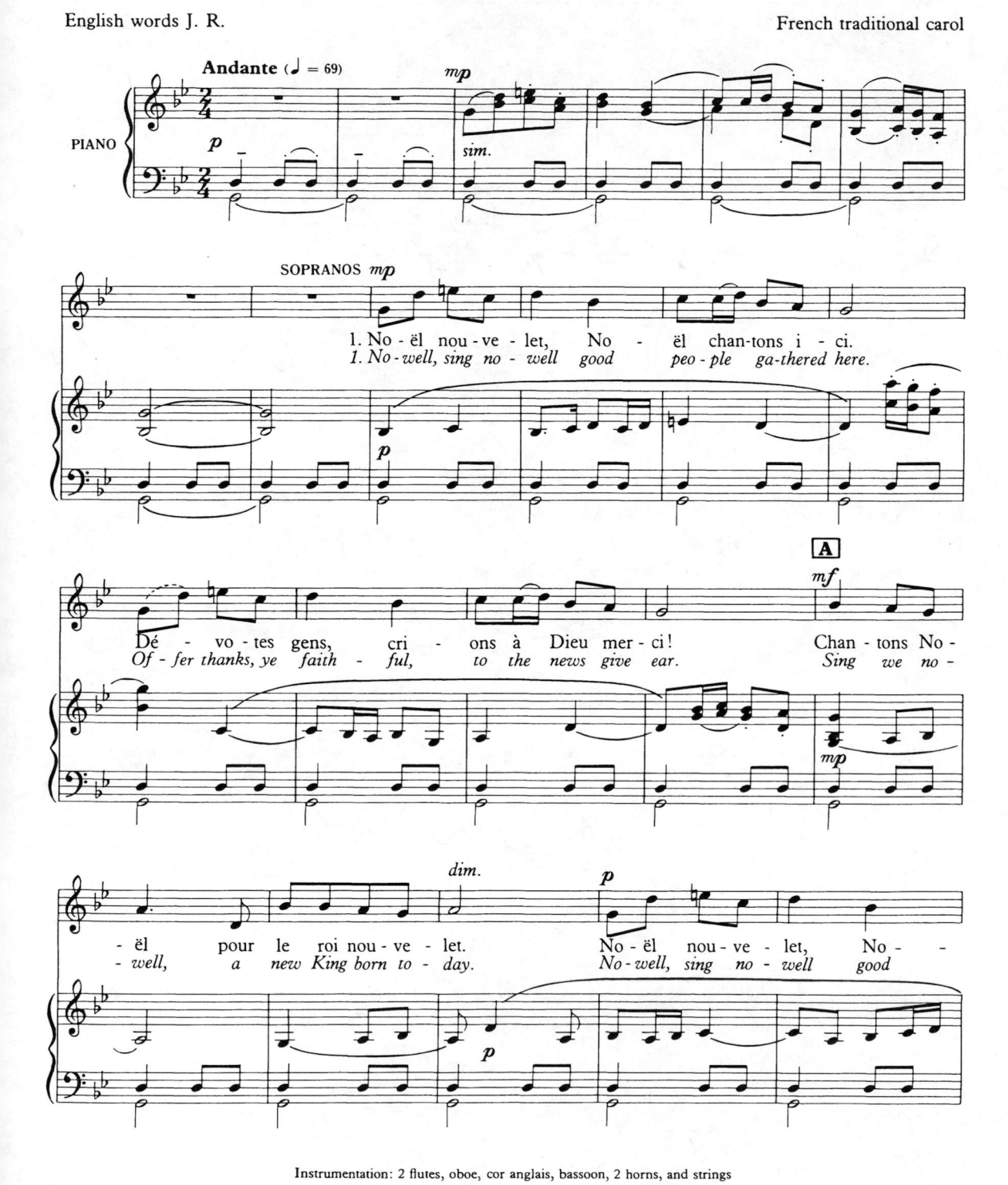

Instrumentation: 2 flutes, oboe, cor anglais, bassoon, 2 horns, and strings

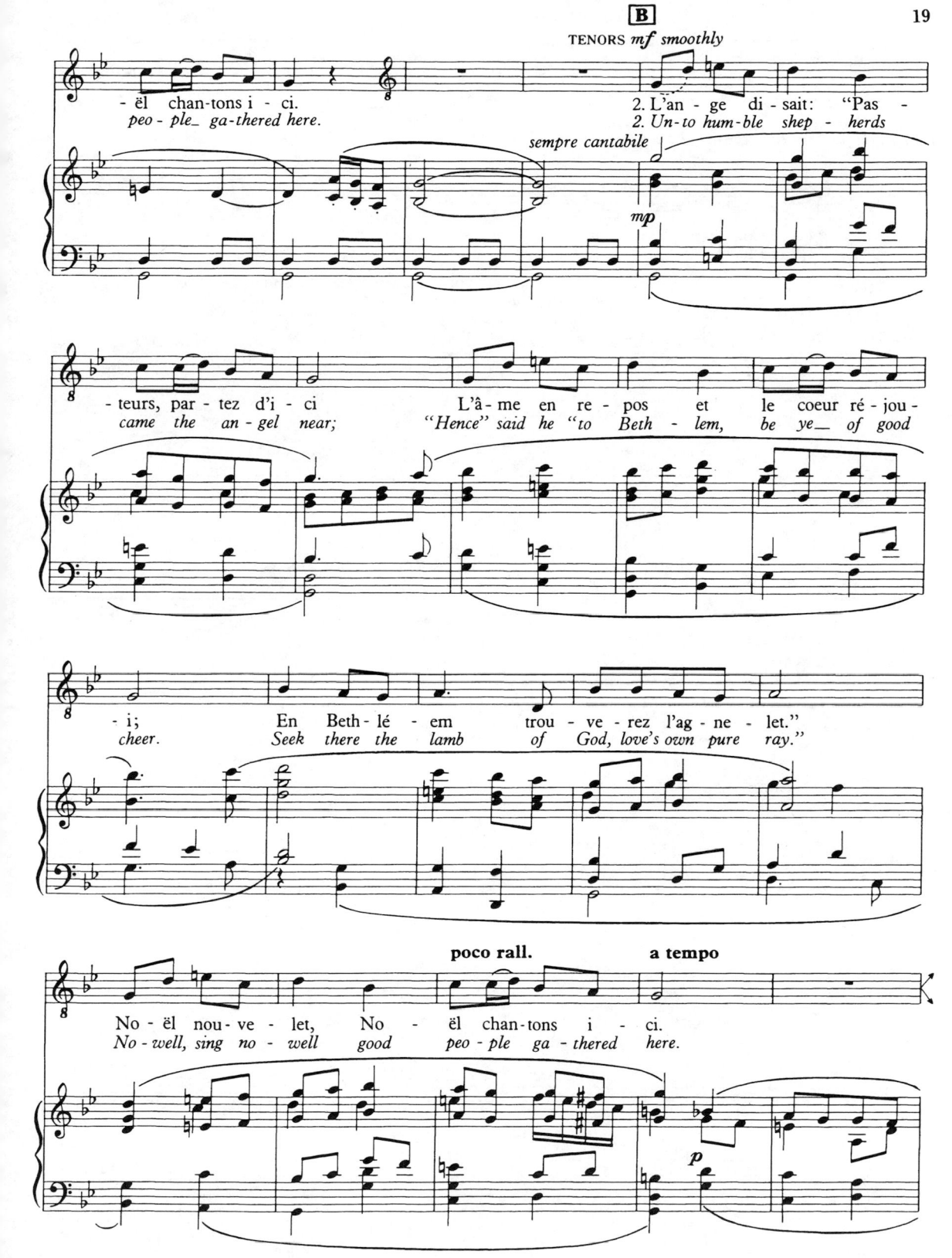
B
TENORS mf smoothly
- ël chan-tons i - ci.
peo - ple_ ga-thered here.
2. L'an - ge di - sait: "Pas -
2. Un-to hum-ble shep - herds
sempre cantabile
mp
- teurs, par - tez d'i - ci
came the an - gel near;
L'â - me en re - pos et le coeur ré - jou -
"Hence" said he "to Beth - lem, be ye_ of good
- i;
cheer.
En Beth - lé - em trou - ve - rez l'ag - ne - let."
Seek there the lamb of God, love's own pure ray."
poco rall.
a tempo
No - ël nou - ve - let, No - ël chan-tons i - ci.
No - well, sing no - well good peo - ple ga - thered here.
p

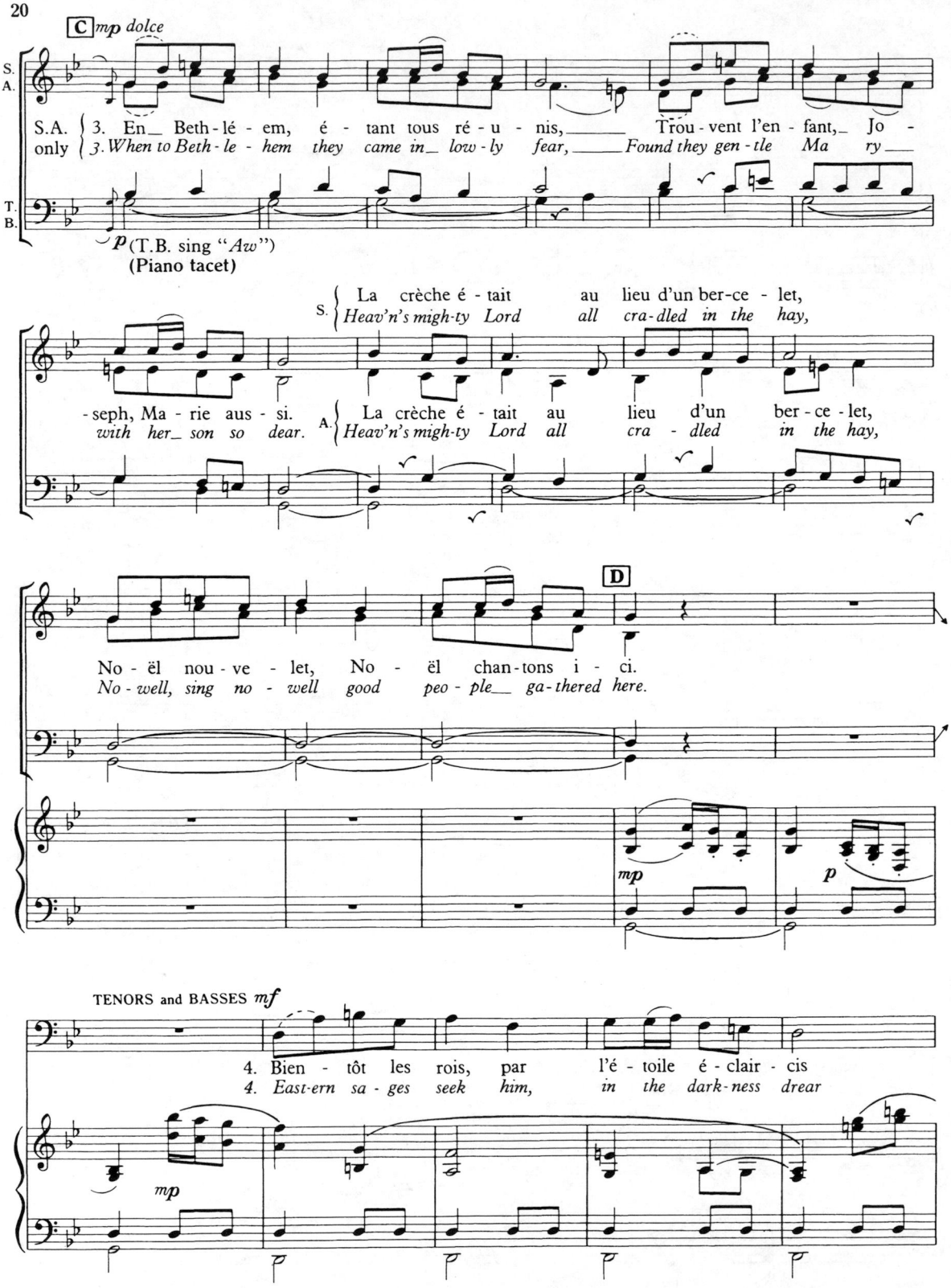
C mp dolce
S.
A.
S.A. only
3. En Beth-lé-em, é-tant tous ré-u-nis, Trou-vent l'en-fant, Jo-
3. When to Beth-le-hem they came in low-ly fear, Found they gen-tle Ma ry
T.
B.
p (T.B. sing "Aw")
(Piano tacet)
S.
La crèche é-tait au lieu d'un ber-ce-let,
Heav'n's migh-ty Lord all cra-dled in the hay,
-seph, Ma-rie aus-si.
with her son so dear.
A.
La crèche é-tait au lieu d'un ber-ce-let,
Heav'n's migh-ty Lord all cra-dled in the hay,
D
No-ël nou-ve-let, No-ël chan-tons i-ci.
No-well, sing no-well good peo-ple ga-thered here.
mp
p
TENORS and BASSES mf
4. Bien-tôt les rois, par l'é-toile é-clair-cis
4. East-ern sa-ges seek him, in the dark-ness drear
mp

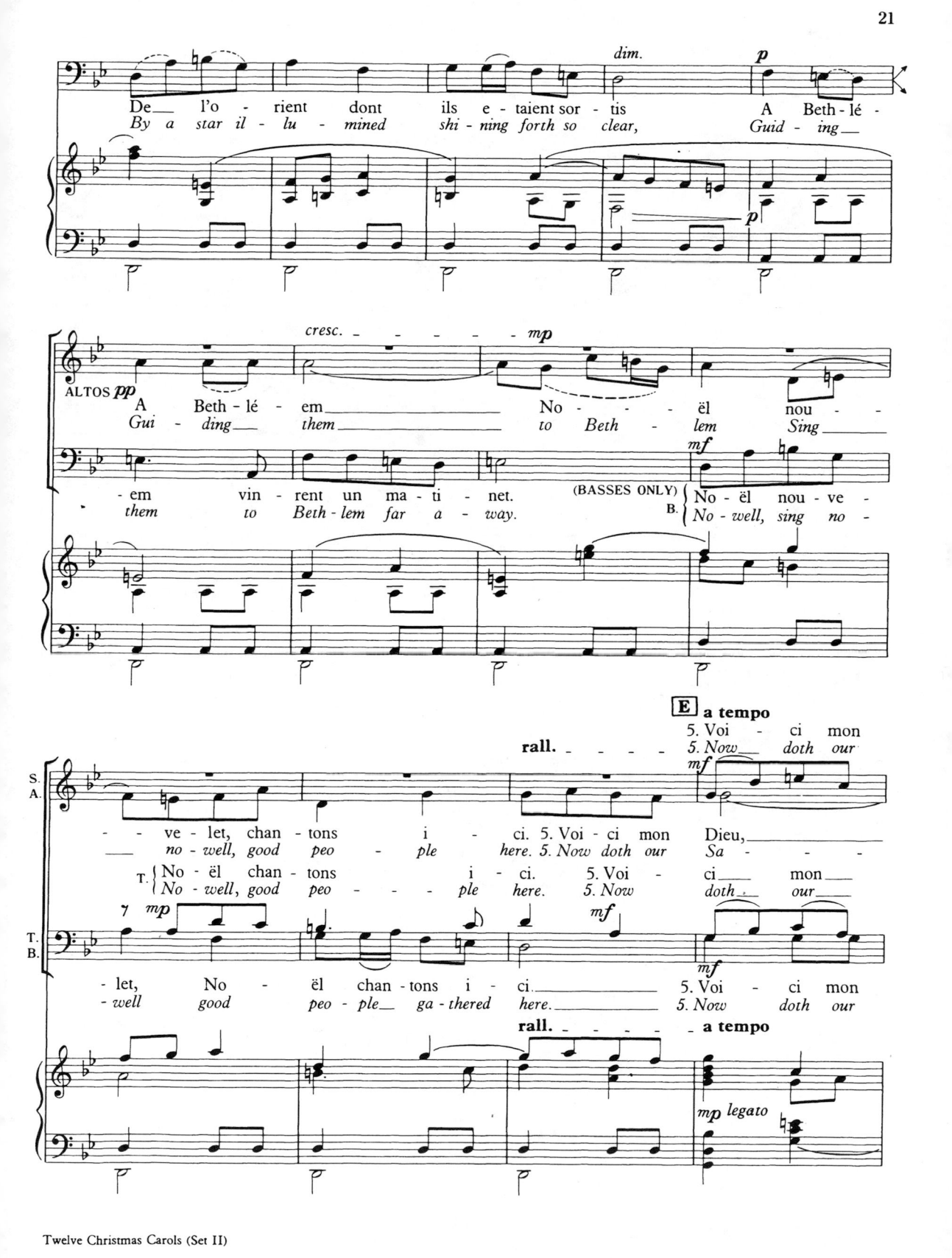
De l'o - rient dont ils e - taient sor - tis A Beth - lé -
By a star il - lu - mined shi - ning forth so clear, Guid - ing
dim.
p
cresc.
mp
ALTOS pp
A Beth - lé - em No - - - ël nou - -
Gui - ding them to Beth - lem Sing
- em vin - rent un ma - ti - net.
them to Beth - lem far a - way.
(BASSES ONLY)
B. No - ël nou - ve -
No - well, sing no -
mf
E a tempo
rall.
5. Voi - ci mon
5. Now doth our
S. A.
- - ve - let, chan - tons i - ci. 5. Voi - ci mon Dieu,
no - well, good peo - ple here. 5. Now doth our Sa - - -
T. No - ël chan - tons i - ci. 5. Voi - ci mon
No - well, good peo - - - ple here. 5. Now doth our
T. B.
- let, No - ël chan - tons i - ci. 5. Voi - ci mon
- well good peo - ple ga - thered here. 5. Now doth our
rall.
a tempo
mp legato

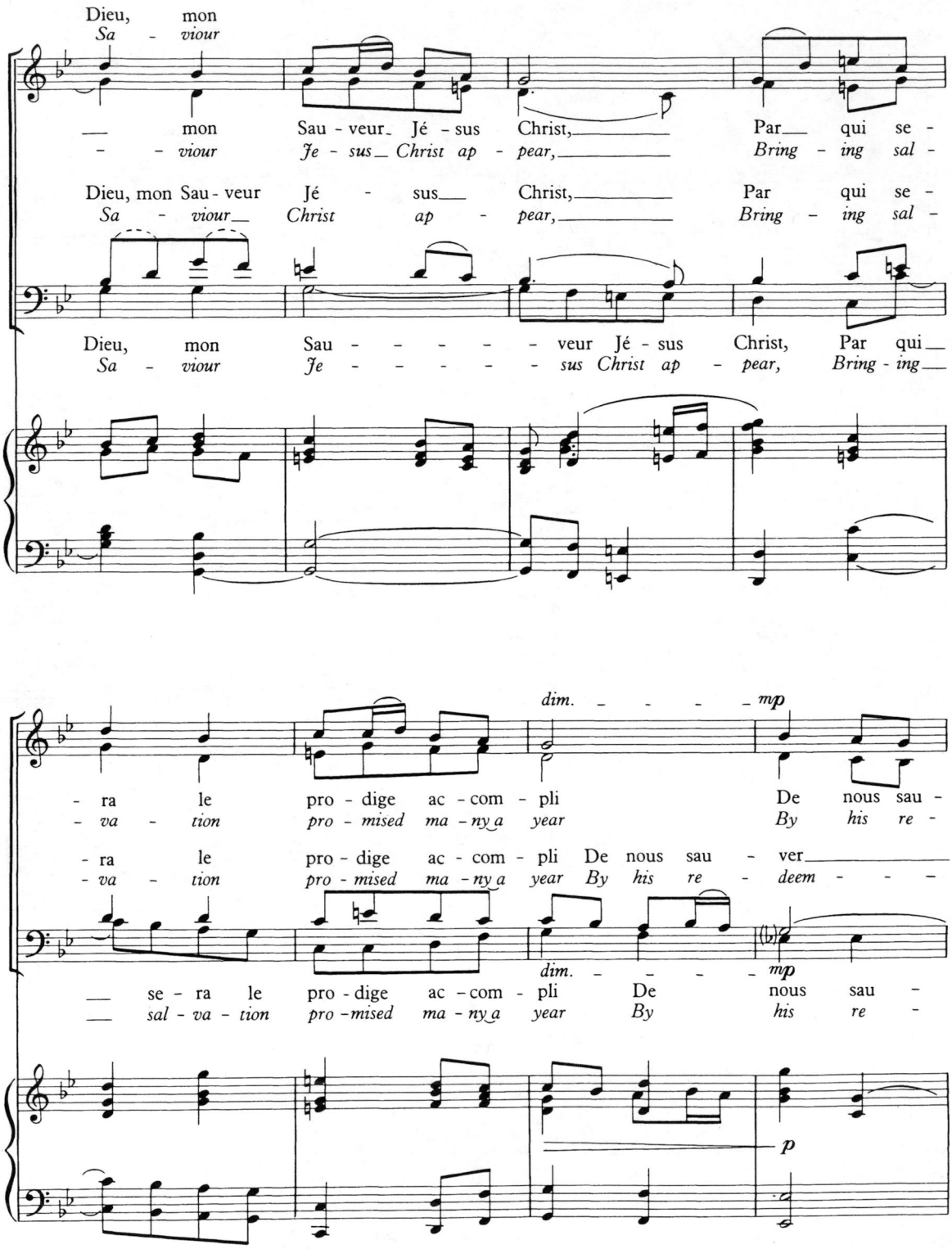
Dieu, mon
Sa - viour
mon Sau - veur Jé - sus Christ, Par qui se -
- viour Je - sus Christ ap - pear, Bring - ing sal -
Dieu, mon Sau - veur Jé - sus Christ, Par qui se -
Sa - viour Christ ap - pear, Bring - ing sal -
Dieu, mon Sau - - - - - veur Jé - sus Christ, Par qui
Sa - viour Je - - - - - sus Christ ap - pear, Bring - ing
dim. - - - - mp
- ra le pro - dige ac - com - pli De nous sau -
- va - tion pro - mised ma - ny a year By his re -
- ra le pro - dige ac - com - pli De nous sau - ver
- va - tion pro - mised ma - ny a year By his re - deem - - -
dim. - - - - mp
se - ra le pro - dige ac - com - pli De nous sau -
sal - va - tion pro - mised ma - ny a year By his re -
p

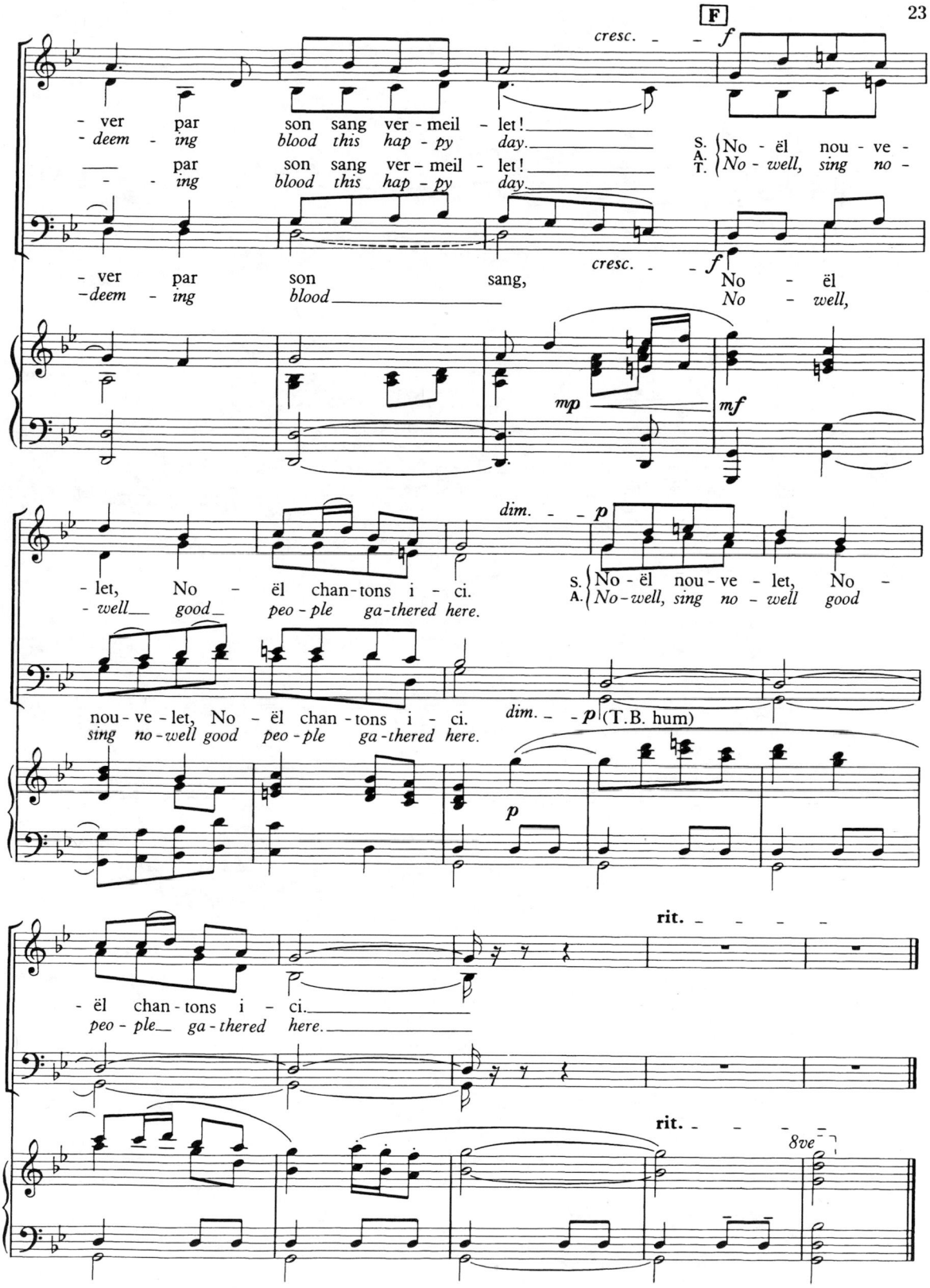
F
cresc.
f
- ver par son sang ver - meil - let!
- deem - ing blood this hap - py day.
par son sang ver - meil - let!
- - ing blood this hap - py day.
S. No - ël nou - ve -
A. No - well, sing no -
T.
- ver par son sang,
-deem - ing blood
No - ël
No - well,
mp
mf
dim.
p
- let, No - ël chan - tons i - ci.
- well good peo - ple ga - thered here.
S. No - ël nou - ve - let, No -
A. No - well, sing no - well good
nou - ve - let, No - ël chan - tons i - ci.
sing no - well good peo - ple ga - thered here.
(T.B. hum)
rit.
- ël chan - tons i - ci.
peo - ple ga - thered here.
8ve

5. SANS DAY CAROL

Cornish traditional carol

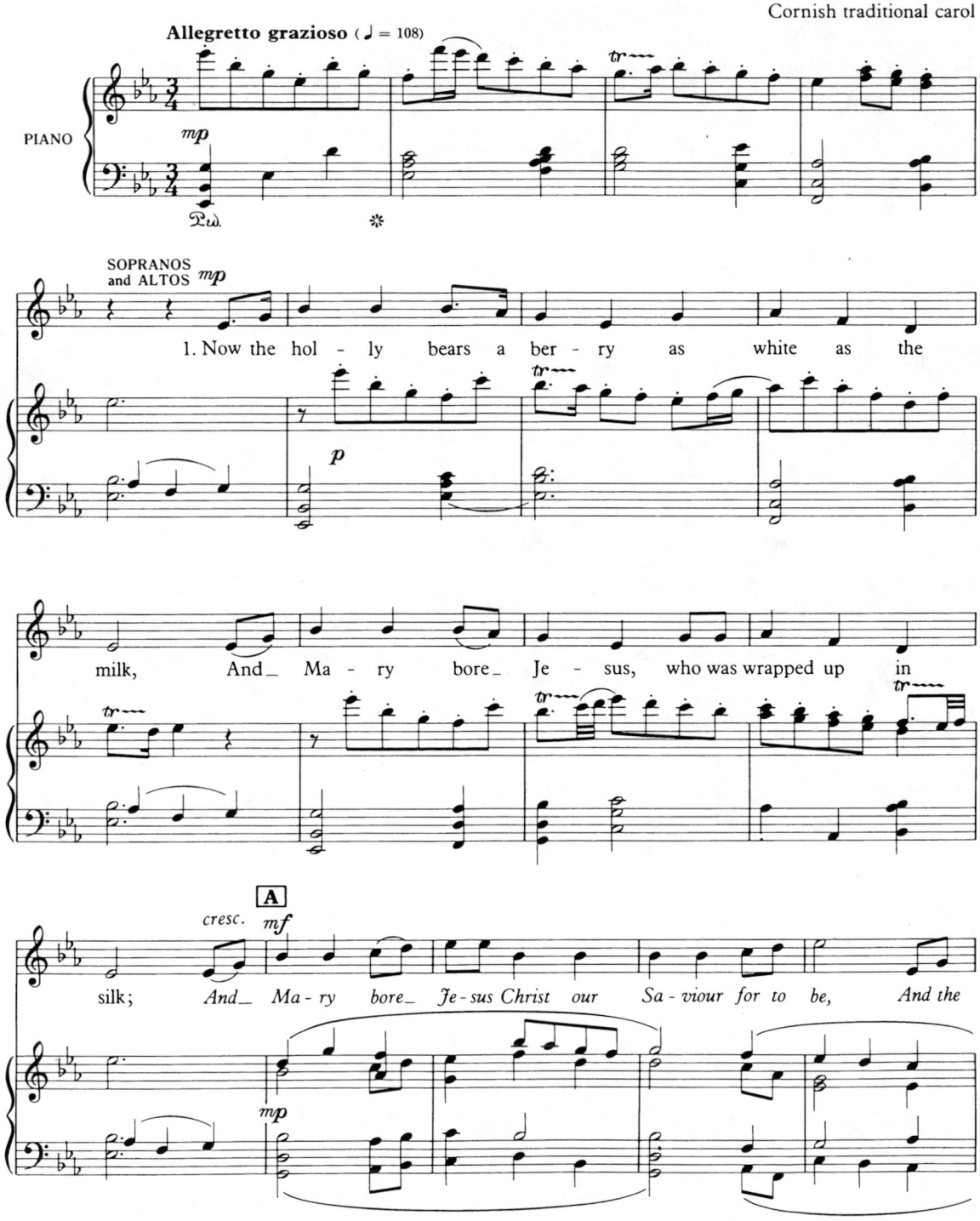

Words collected by Percy Dearmer and used by permission of Oxford University Press
Instrumentation: 2 flutes (1 doubling piccolo), 2 oboes, bassoon, 2 horns, and strings.

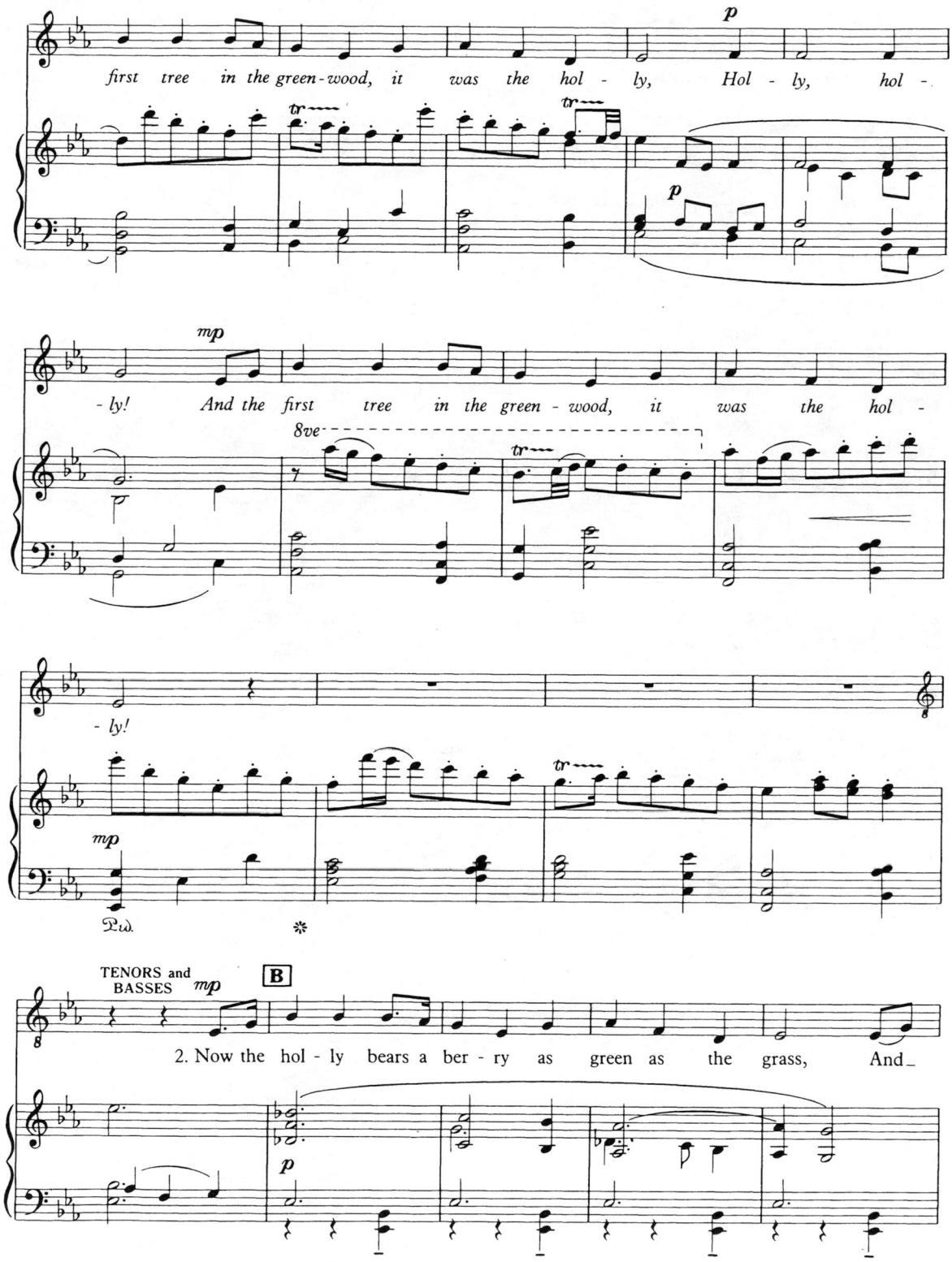
p
first tree in the green-wood, it was the hol - ly, Hol - ly, hol -
tr
tr
p
mp
- ly! And the first tree in the green - wood, it was the hol -
8ve
tr
- ly!
mp
Ped.
TENORS and BASSES
mp
B
2. Now the hol - ly bears a ber - ry as green as the grass, And
p

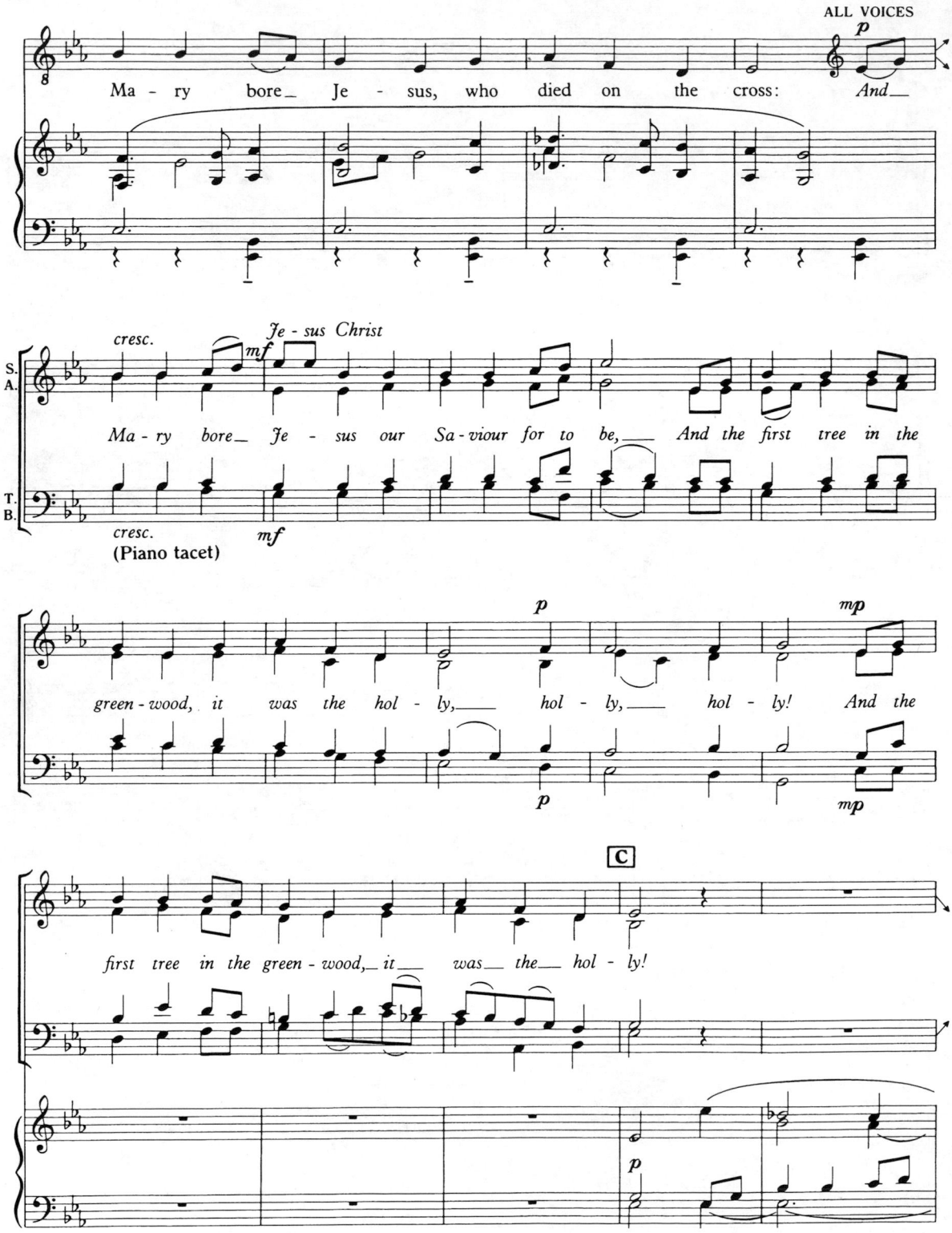
ALL VOICES
p
Ma - ry bore Je - sus, who died on the cross: And
cresc.
mf
Je - sus Christ
S.
A.
Ma - ry bore Je - sus our Sa - viour for to be, And the first tree in the
T.
B.
cresc.
mf
(Piano tacet)
p
mp
green - wood, it was the hol - ly, hol - ly, hol - ly! And the
p
mp
C
first tree in the green - wood, it was the hol - ly!
p

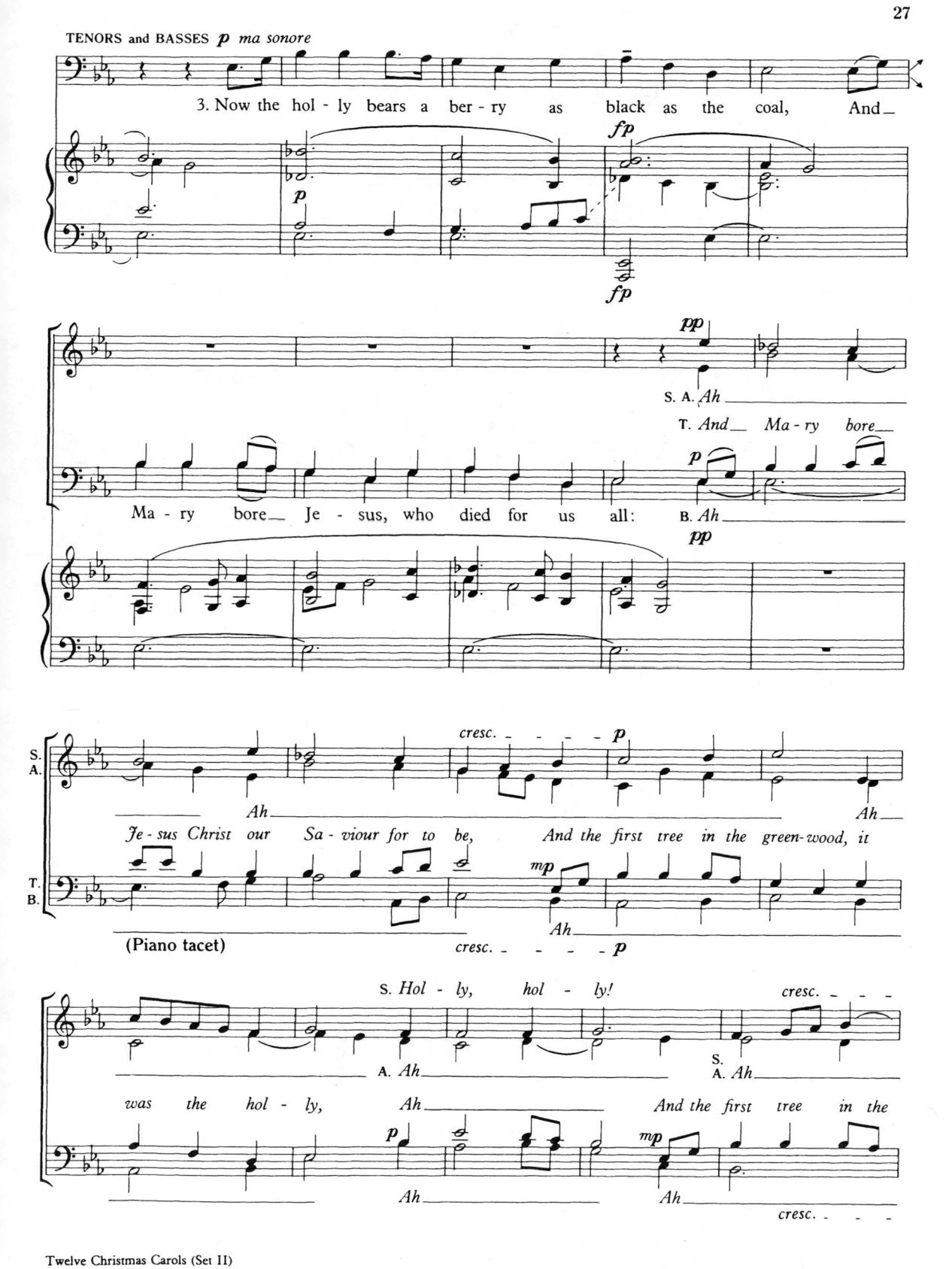
TENORS and BASSES p ma sonore
3. Now the hol - ly bears a ber - ry as black as the coal, And
fp
p
fp
pp
S. A. Ah
T. And Ma - ry bore
Ma - ry bore Je - sus, who died for us all:
p
B. Ah
pp
S. A.
cresc.
p
Ah
Ah
Je - sus Christ our Sa - viour for to be, And the first tree in the green-wood, it
T. B.
mp
Ah
(Piano tacet)
cresc.
p
S. Hol - ly, hol - ly!
cresc.
A. Ah
S. A. Ah
was the hol - ly, Ah And the first tree in the
p
mp
Ah
Ah
cresc.

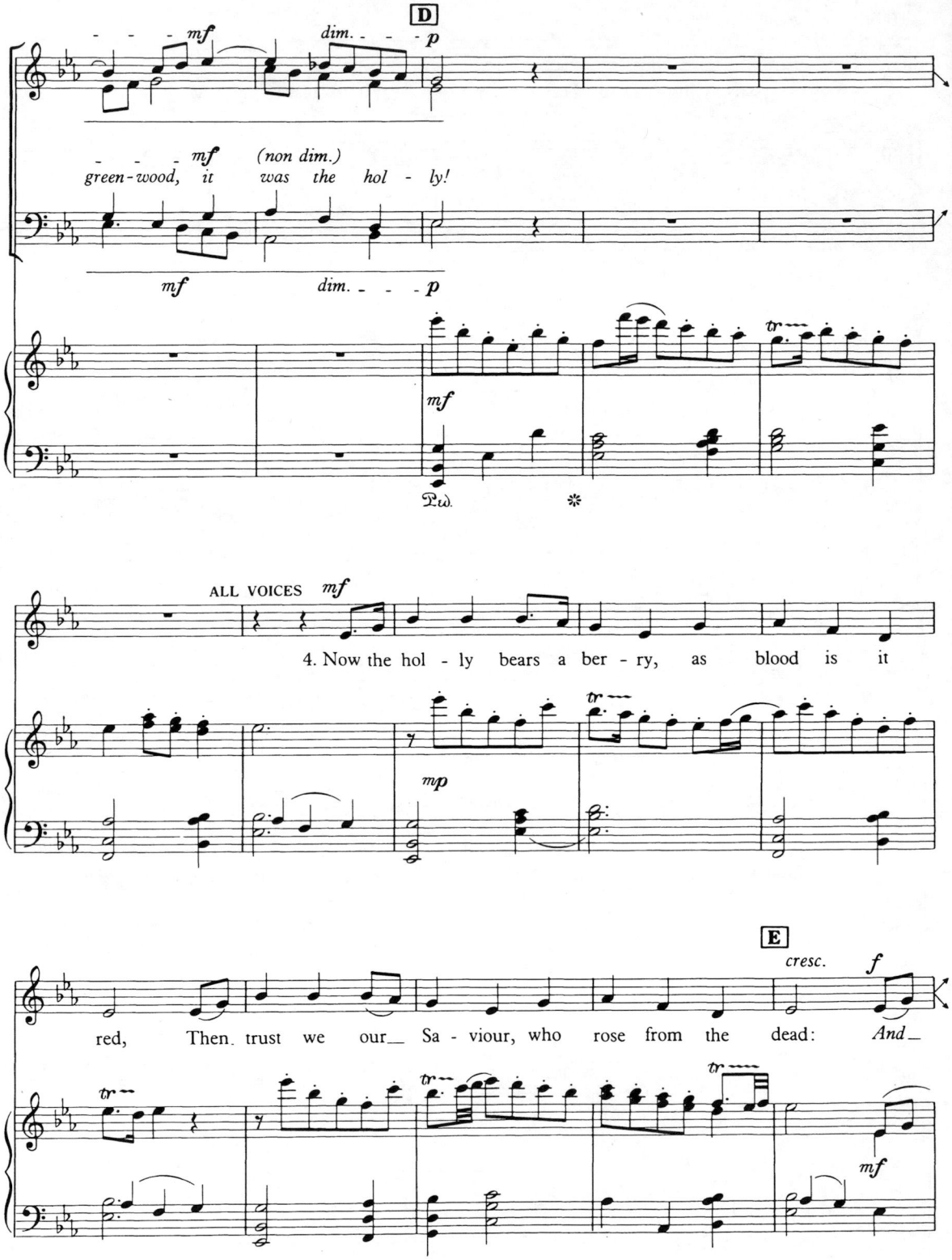
D
mf
dim.
p
green-wood, it was the hol - ly!
mf
(non dim.)
mf
dim.
p
mf
Ped.
ALL VOICES
mf
4. Now the hol - ly bears a ber - ry, as blood is it
mp
E
cresc.
f
red, Then trust we our Sa - viour, who rose from the dead: And
mf

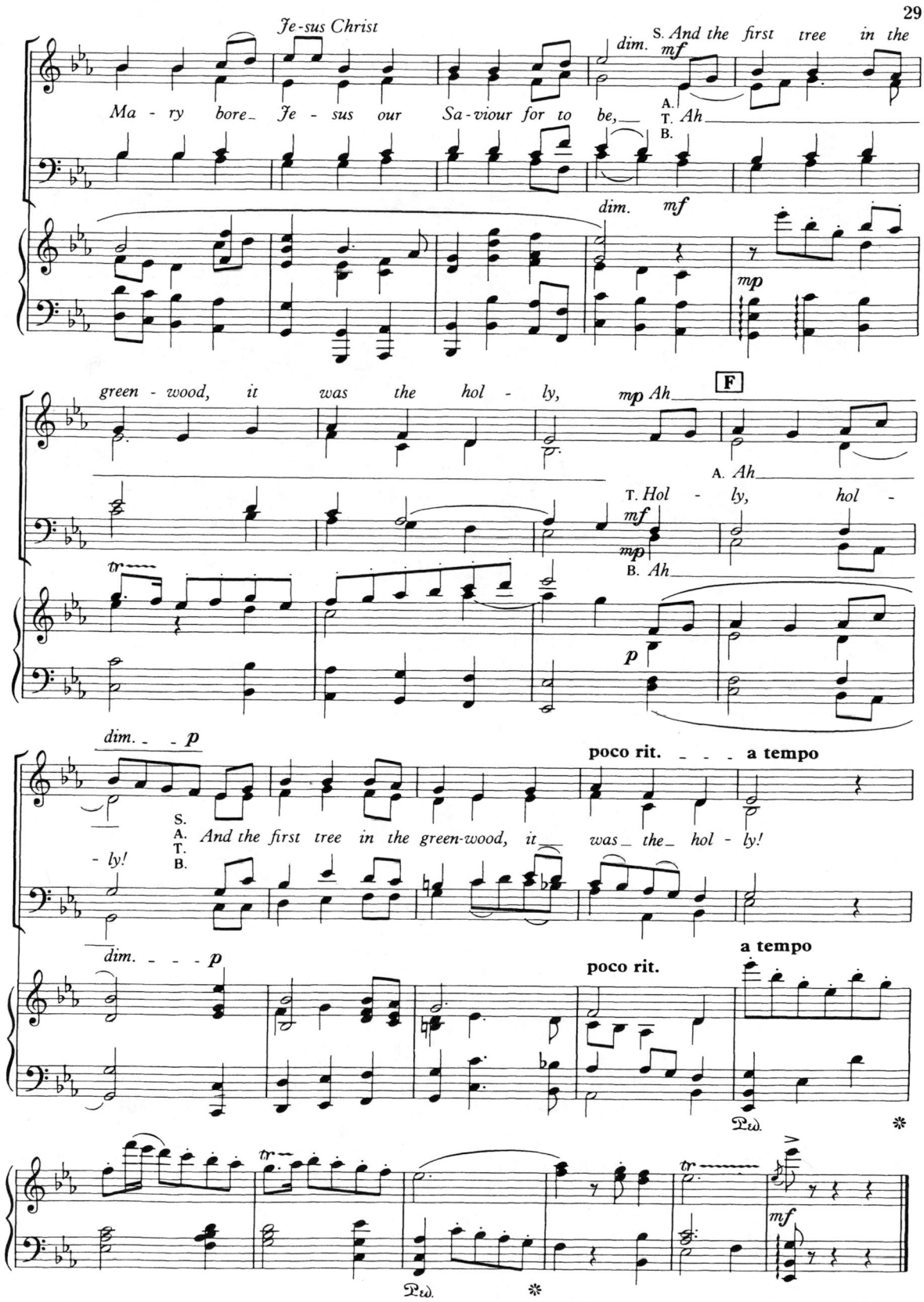
Je-sus Christ
Ma - ry bore Je - sus our Sa-viour for to be,
S. And the first tree in the
A. T. B. Ah
dim.
mf
mp
green - wood, it was the hol - ly,
mp Ah
F
A. Ah
T. Hol - ly, hol -
mf
mp
B. Ah
tr
p
dim. p
poco rit. a tempo
S. A. T. B. And the first tree in the green-wood, it was the hol - ly!
- ly!
dim. p
poco rit.
a tempo
Ped.
*
tr
mf

6. THE COMING OF OUR KING

Words anon. Polish traditional carol

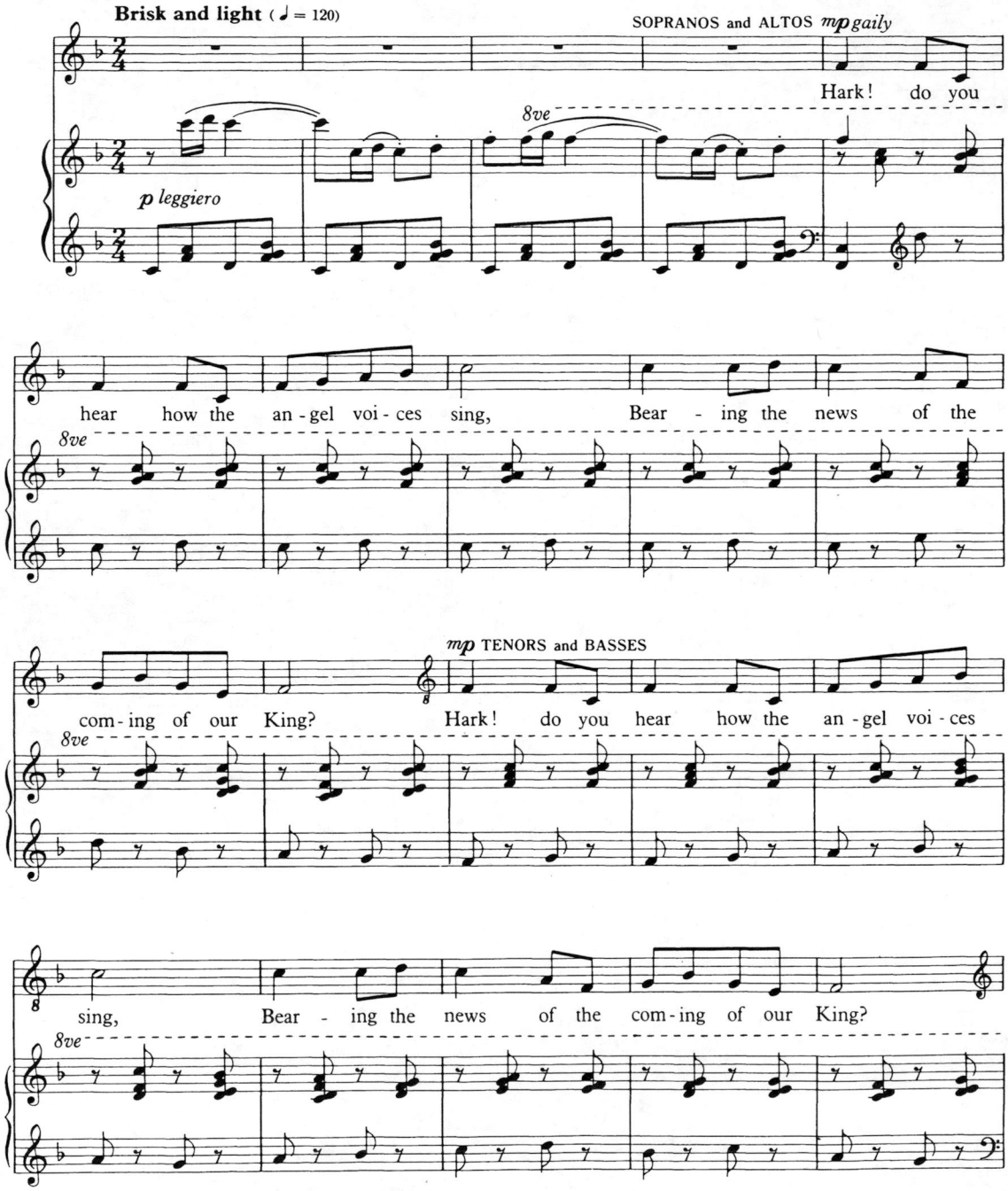

Instrumentation: 2 flutes, 2 oboes, bassoon, 2 horns, glockenspiel, harp (opt.), and strings

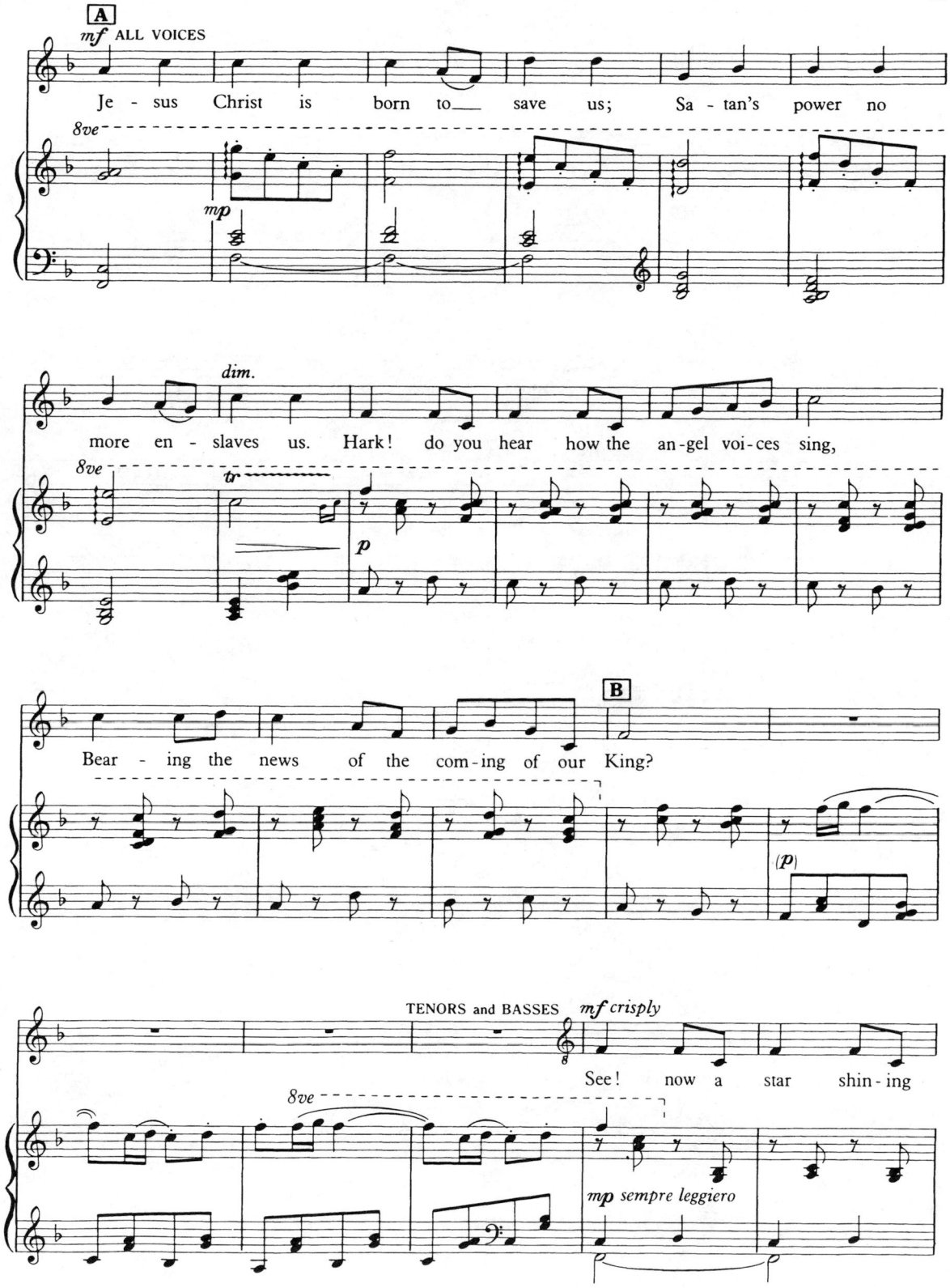
A
mf ALL VOICES
Je - sus Christ is born to save us; Sa - tan's power no
8ve
mp
dim.
more en - slaves us. Hark! do you hear how the an-gel voi-ces sing,
8ve
tr
p
B
Bear - ing the news of the com-ing of our King?
(p)
TENORS and BASSES
mf crisply
See! now a star shin-ing
8ve
mp sempre leggiero

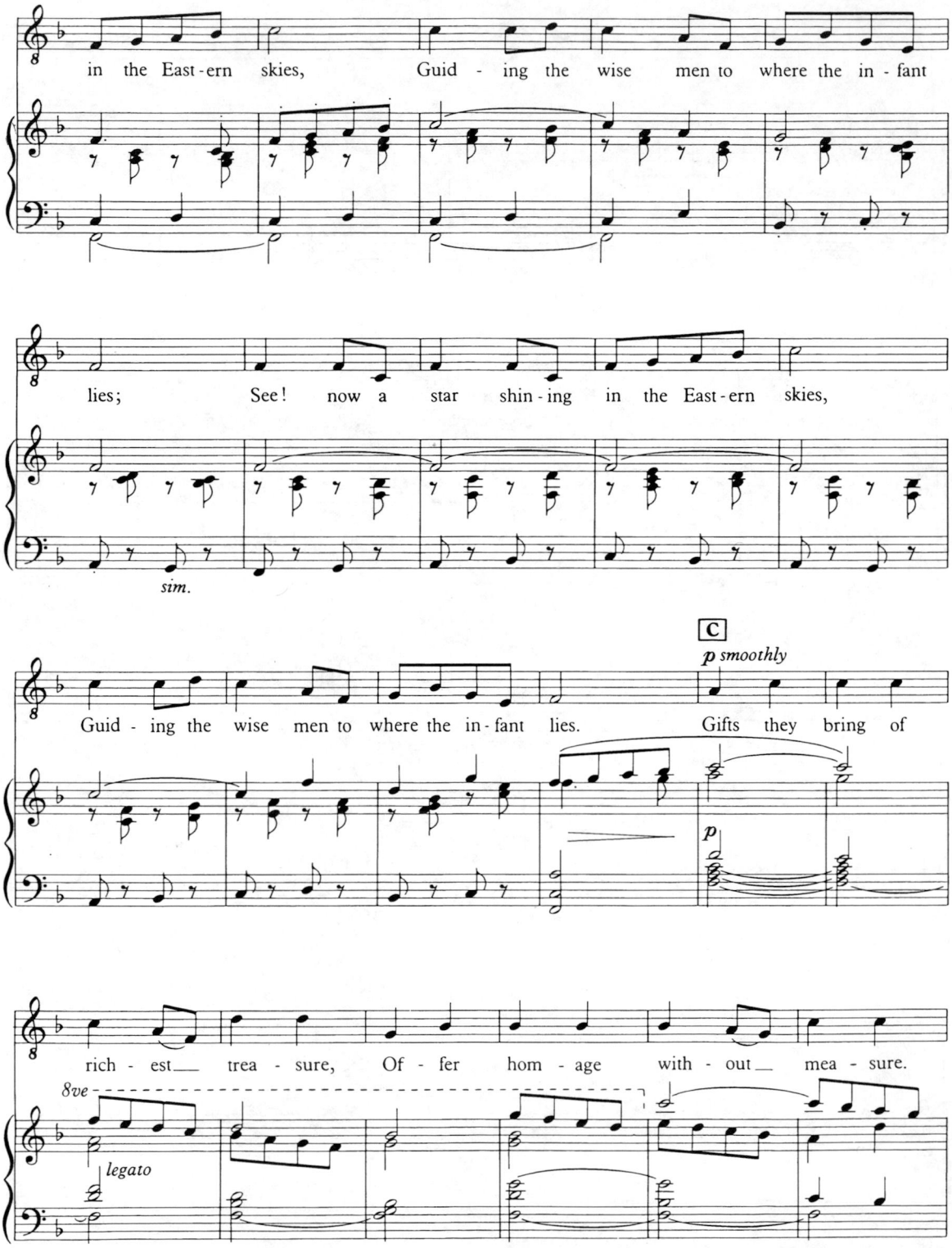
in the East-ern skies, Guid - ing the wise men to where the in - fant
lies; See! now a star shin - ing in the East-ern skies,
sim.
C
p smoothly
Guid - ing the wise men to where the in - fant lies. Gifts they bring of
p
rich - est trea - sure, Of - fer hom - age with - out mea - sure.
8ve
legato

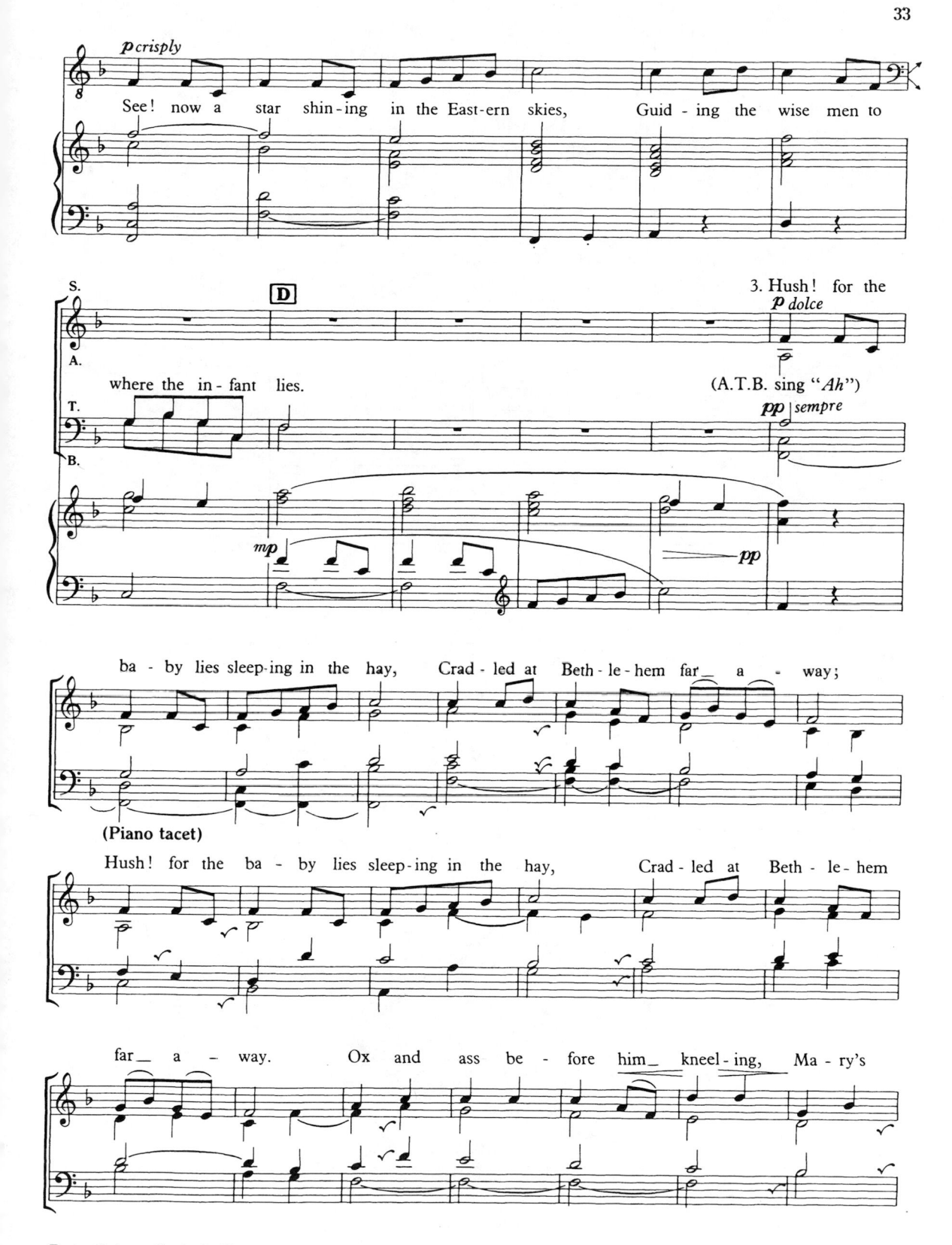
p crisply
See! now a star shin-ing in the East-ern skies, Guid-ing the wise men to
S.
A.
T.
B.
D
where the in-fant lies.
3. Hush! for the
p dolce
(A.T.B. sing "Ah")
pp sempre
mp
pp
ba-by lies sleep-ing in the hay, Crad-led at Beth-le-hem far a-way;
(Piano tacet)
Hush! for the ba-by lies sleep-ing in the hay, Crad-led at Beth-le-hem
far a-way. Ox and ass be-fore him kneel-ing, Ma-ry's

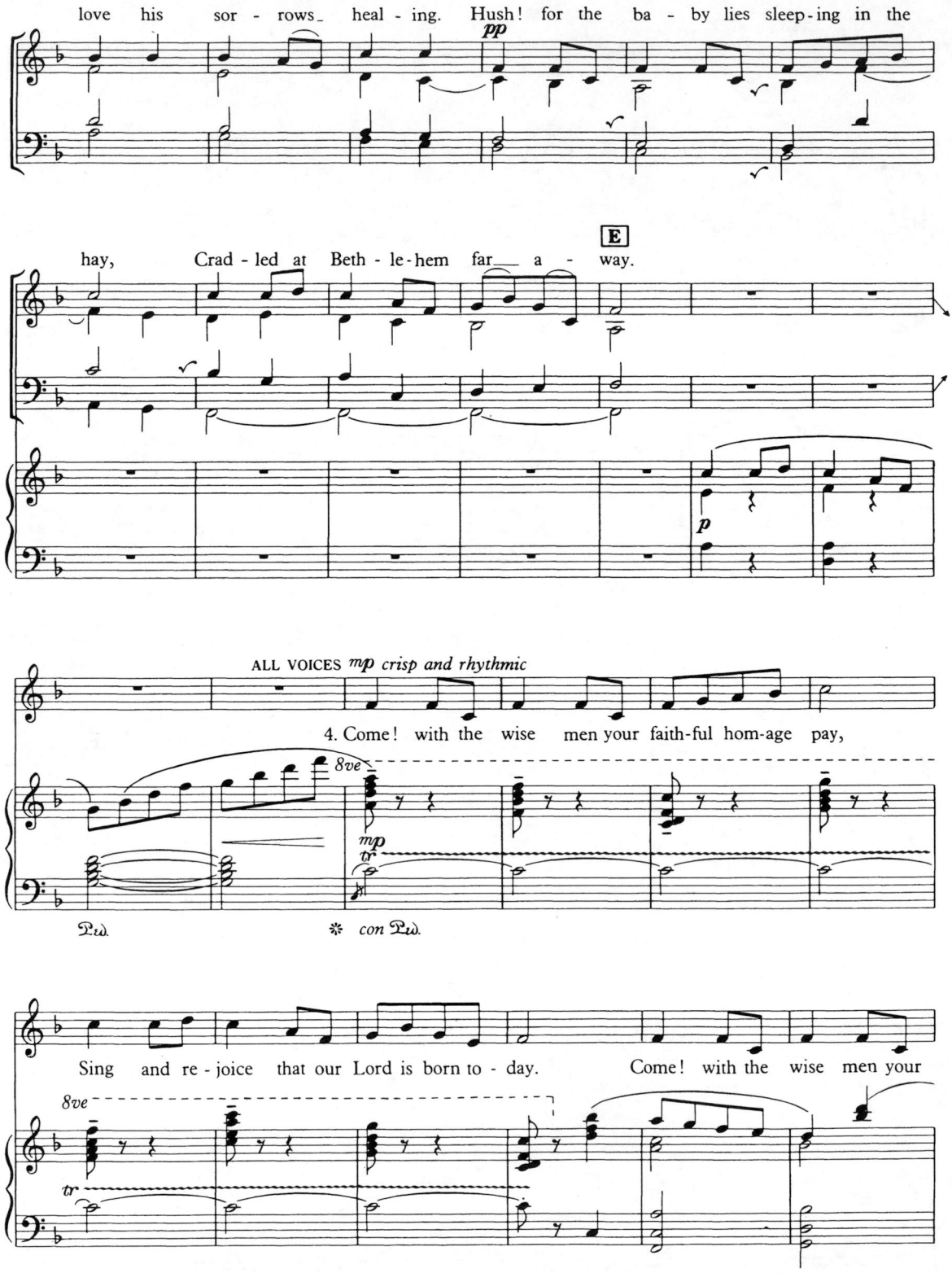
love his sor - rows heal - ing. Hush! for the ba - by lies sleep - ing in the
pp
hay, Crad - led at Beth - le - hem far a - way.
E
p
ALL VOICES mp crisp and rhythmic
4. Come! with the wise men your faith-ful hom-age pay,
8ve
mp
tr
con
Sing and re - joice that our Lord is born to - day. Come! with the wise men your
8ve
tr

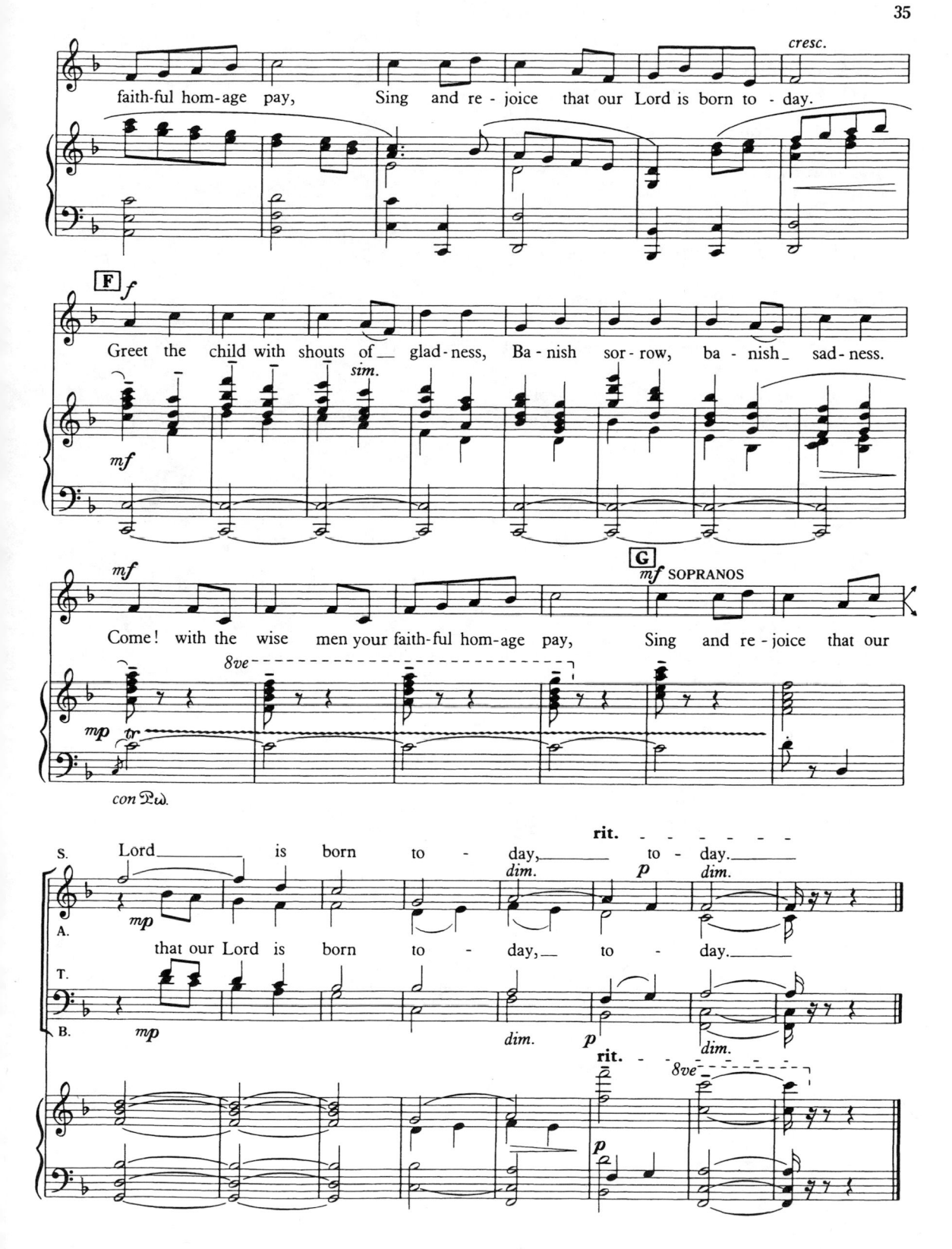
cresc.
faith-ful hom-age pay, Sing and re - joice that our Lord is born to - day.
F
f
Greet the child with shouts of glad-ness, Ba - nish sor - row, ba - nish sad-ness.
sim.
mf
mf
G
mf SOPRANOS
Come! with the wise men your faith-ful hom-age pay, Sing and re - joice that our
8ve
mp
tr
con 𝔓𝔞.
rit.
S. Lord is born to - day, to - day.
dim.
p
dim.
A.
mp
that our Lord is born to - day, to - day.
T.
B.
mp
dim.
p
dim.
rit.
8ve
p

OXFORD CHRISTMAS COLLECTIONS

100 Carols for Choirs
edited and arranged by David Willcocks and John Rutter

Carols for Choirs 1

Carols for Choirs 2

Carols for Choirs 3

Carols for Choirs 4 (upper voices)

The New Oxford Book of Carols
201 carols, supplemented with extensive notes on historical background and performance, edited by Hugh Keyte and Andrew Parrott. Available in hardback and paperback.

The Shorter New Oxford Book of Carols
122 carols selected from *The New Oxford Book of Carols*, edited by Hugh Keyte and Andrew Parrott

Oxford Choral Classics: Christmas Motets
Sixteen motets selected and edited by John Rutter

The Oxford Book of Carols
197 carols edited by Percy Dearmer, Ralph Vaughan Williams, and Martin Shaw

A Little Carol Book
Fifteen Christmas carols and hymns arranged for mixed voices by John Rutter
Not for sale in the USA

Eight Christmas Carols
in two sets, arranged for mixed voices and small orchestra or piano by John Rutter

Six Carols with Descants
arranged for mixed voices and organ by Philip Ledger

Twelve Christmas Carols
in two sets, arranged for mixed voices and small orchestra or piano by John Rutter

Please write for our catalogue of Oxford Christmas Music which details carol collections for schools, carol orchestrations, individual carols, and other music for Christmas including choral works, nativity plays, and instrumental music.

OXFORD
UNIVERSITY PRESS

www.oup.com

ISBN 978-0-19-385022-4